D1565382

When Your Children Marry

When Your Children Marry

How Marriage Changes Relationships with Sons and Daughters

Deborah M. Merrill

ROWMAN & LITTLEFIELD PUBLISHERS, INC.
Lanham • Boulder • New York • Toronto • Plymouth, UK

Published by Rowman & Littlefield Publishers, Inc.
A wholly owned subsidiary of The Rowman & Littlefield Publishing Group, Inc.
4501 Forbes Boulevard, Suite 200, Lanham, Maryland 20706
http://www.rowmanlittlefield.com

Estover Road, Plymouth PL6 7PY, United Kingdom

British Library Cataloguing in Publication Information Available

Library of Congress Cataloging-in-Publication Data

Merrill, Deborah M., 1962–
  When your children marry : how marriage changes relationships with sons and
daughters / Deborah M. Merrill.
    p. cm.
  Includes bibliographical references and index.
  ISBN 978-1-4422-1092-9 (cloth : alk. paper) ISBN 978-1-4422-1094-3 (electronic)
  1. Marriage. 2. Parent and adult child. 3. Intergenerational relations. 4. Alternative
lifestyles. I. Title.
  HQ519.M47 2011
  306.874—dc22   2010054121

∞™ The paper used in this publication meets the minimum requirements of American
National Standard for Information Sciences—Permanence of Paper for Printed Library
Materials, ANSI/NISO Z39.48-1992.

Printed in the United States of America

This book is dedicated to my mother,

Nancy Lane Merrill,

and to the memory of my father,

Justin S. Merrill,

for all of their love and support.

It is also dedicated to my mother-in-law,

Rosalie M. Smith,

who has always encouraged my career,

to my father-in-law and his wife,

Dr. Charles E. and Glenda B. Basye,

who are like second parents to me,

and to the memory of Lynda S. Basye.

Contents

viii   *Contents*

Acknowledgments

This research would not have been possible without the support of a Faculty Research Grant from Clark University for 2008–2009. This financial assistance allowed me to interview all of the mothers, daughters, and sons for this study. An interview stipend not only piques the interest of the public; it also legitimates the importance of the study and the credibility of the researcher. I am most grateful to Clark for this assistance. Thanks also to all of the sons, daughters, and mothers for sharing their time and the details of their family lives. It is a privilege to hear people's deepest feelings about and insights into their families. I do not take this privilege lightly.

I would also like to acknowledge Nancy Budwig, dean of research at Clark University; David Angel, prior provost and current president of Clark University; and colleague Patricia Ewick for their support and encouragement of my research. It was Nancy and Patty who pushed me out of a slump several years ago and helped me to turn my research profile around. David and Nancy continued to encourage this last book for which I am grateful. Clark is a very special university, and I am honored to be a part of it.

Acknowledgment also goes to the members of the Sociology Department at Clark University: Parminder Bhachu, Melissa Butler, Patricia Ewick, Sheila Hokanson, Bruce London, Debra Osnowitz, Robert J. S. Ross, and Shelly Tenenbaum. I thank them for giving a rookie teacher a shot and for their continued friendship and intellectual exchanges over the years. I would particularly like to thank Shelly Tenenbaum and Patty Ewick for their willingness to help me in planning my career trajectory; they are truly exceptional colleagues. A special thanks also goes to Sheila Hokanson for so efficiently handling the department's day-to-day challenges and for, quite frankly, putting up with me.

I would also like to acknowledge my mentors and colleagues who have helped me along the way. Liliane Floge and Craig McEwen sparked my interest in sociology while an undergraduate at Bowdoin College. Linda Waite and Fran Goldscheider further piqued and deepened that interest and initiated my career in family sociology and demography. Since then, Vern Bengtson, Ingrid Connidis, Calvin Goldscheider, Leora Lawton, Anne Martin Matthews, Sarah Matthews, Phyllis Moen, Karl Pillemer, Merril Silverstein, Glenna Spitze, J. Jill Suitor, and Natalia Sarkisian have provided assistance, encouragement, or inspiration along the way. I thank them for all of the work that they have done in the study of parents and adult children. A special thanks goes to Glenna Spitze for her willingness to read an earlier section of this work.

I also thank my friends who hear more about this topic than is humane, including but not limited to: Aimee Basye, Marcia Butzel, Nina Kushner, Pat Little, Kevin and Martha McKenna, Amy Richter, Valerie Sperling, Mark Turnbull, and Kristen Williams. Special thanks to Molly and Gracie for their love and trust. Gracie provided constant companionship while I worked on the book from the onset of the idea through the first draft, a true friend indeed.

Last, but not least, I thank my partner and husband, Ken Basye, for enriching my life, and the students at Clark University, who make it all worthwhile. This book would not be possible without you.

Introduction

> A daughter is a daughter all of her life, but a son is a son 'til he
> takes him a wife.

$\mathscr{I}$ do not remember the first time that I heard this adage. It certainly was not something that my parents said or believed in. They were both very close to their own parents; my father was as devoted a son as my mother was a daughter. However, it was a script for the American middle-class family that I knew as well as any other. Daughters are expected to stay close to their family even after marriage. Sons, on the other hand, are assumed to "trade off" being a son for a husband. The how and why, though, are not expressed in that script. Does the husband trade having a wife and children for his place in his parental family? Why don't wives do that, and is this the actual reality of today's families? Although I first heard of this maxim as a young child, it wasn't until I was married myself and a daughter-in-law that I questioned the fairness of this practice, the extent of its existence, and its implications for families and intergenerational relationships.

The genesis of this book is several-fold. It is partly personal. My husband and I see more of my family than my husband's family. I have always assumed, and perhaps even have rationalized, that this is because my family lives nearby and my husband's family is on the other side of the country. I question, however, if I would accept this same situation if it were my family that lived far away. I also ask how common my own experience is and why other couples spend more time with one side of the family than the other.

My interest in how marriage transforms parent–adult child relationships is also an intellectual one. My scholarship has focused on intergenerational relationships, parent–adult child bonds, and the myriad factors that affect them. More recently I have turned my attention to in-law relationships, specifically mother-in-law and daughter-in-law relationships.[1] My findings suggest that, indeed, the nature of the mother-son relationship has a profound effect on the relationship between mother-in-law and daughter-in-law. Readers commenting on *Salon*'s website, however, argued that the findings of my book suggest a double standard for men versus women.[2] Specifically, while women are allowed and expected to remain close to their parents following marriage, men are expected to "cut the cord." I decided to investigate whether or not we really do have this expectation of a son's diminished role in his natal family following marriage and just how common it is.

Relationships between parents and adult children are generally positive with typically relative proximity, frequent contact, and emotional closeness.[3] However, conflict is often present as well. The coexistence of both sentiments simultaneously, referred to as ambivalence, occurs for both parents and children. It is more common for mothers than for fathers, however.[4] In addition, parents tend to report more positive relationships than their children, particularly on measures of closeness.[5] Women are also more involved than men in maintaining intergenerational relationships across adulthood. In fact, the mother-daughter bond is the closest of all of the dyads.[6]

Intergenerational relationships are not static, however. They are instead affected by a variety of life course transitions, including marriage. Gender plays a significant mediating role. Relationships with both parents improve for women when they marry, while single men have a better relationship with their mother than do married men.[7] This book will look in depth at why marriage differentially changes relationships with sons versus daughters. Marriage is a particularly important life course event to consider, since it alters the balance of preexisting relationships in the natal family and challenges the notion of who is family. Changes in relationships are due both to the gendered nature of parent–adult child bonds and the social construction of marriage. The focus of this book is on how these social constructions matter.

Among other changes, contact with parents following marriage tends to differ for daughters versus sons. Women have more visits and phone contact with their parents than do men. Men also talk on the phone with their in-laws more than women.[8] Couples are also more responsive to the needs of the wife's parents and are less likely to exclude her parents from care when both sets of parents need care.[9] The question remains, though, whether or not the *couple* as a whole has more contact with the wife's side of the family, and if so, what men's perspectives are as to how and why this occurs. It has been suggested that men get "pulled in" to their wife's side of the family.[10] If that is so, what is the process by which this occurs and how is this related to the adage, "a son is a son 'til he takes him a wife?" What is it about the gendered nature of intergenerational ties that makes the couple stay closer to the wife's family than to the husband's family? These questions will be addressed here.

The final impetus for writing this book is my interest in the institution of marriage. I have closely followed the debate on marriage over the years: the importance and significance of marriage as an institution versus a personal arrangement, the costs and benefits of marriage for men versus women, the history and change in the meaning of marriage, and the possibility of marriage becoming just another alternative living arrangement. Sociologists Coser and Coser were among the first to characterize modern marriage as a "greedy institution," one that demands the undivided commitment of both husband and wife.[11] More recently, others have argued that marriage undermines intergenerational relationships, showing how divorced children have lower levels of integration with parents than the never married, but higher levels than the married. They find that this is true for both men and women even when controlling for differences in time demands, needs and resources, and demographics and extended family composition.[12]

What is it about marriage that makes it a greedy institution? Historian Stephanie Coontz argues that "traditional" marriage, prior to industrialization, was based on an alliance between families to share land, power, and other resources.[13] With industrialization, young adults no longer depended on their parents for independence, and love became the basis of "companionate" marriages. Couples married for companionship and to raise a family; they stayed together as long as they continued to love one another. Today, though, couples also expect self-fulfillment in their marriages. They look toward marriage to enhance their well-being and to aid them in aspiring to their greatest potential. Marital partners are expected to be best friends and to find fulfillment in one another more than ever before.

Not coincidentally, the rise in "individualized" marriages coincided with the increase in the divorce rate from the 1960s through the early 1980s. Couples ended those marriages in which they did not find self-fulfillment. During this time, however, the symbolic significance of marriage increased. No longer something that just anybody could sustain, marriage became a coveted status and the capstone of one's adulthood.[14] It marked the ability to live independently and meant one had "made it" as an adult.

In this book, I will argue that marriage has become increasingly greedy because of the expectation that individualistic marriages must produce self-fulfillment and the enhanced symbolic significance of marriage. Marriage is no longer one of many sources of self-fulfillment; it is *the* source for adults. In fact, it is the most important of all adult relationships, masking even the importance of parenthood. Likewise, the nuclear family is expected to be an independent and self-sustaining entity that is no longer dependent on the broader nuclear family. Its independence and presumed privacy are in fact sacred. As a result of these changes, men and women expect more of their spouse. They expect to be best friends and the focus of one another's lives. Time, defined now in terms of minutes and seconds rather than days and hours, is more precious than ever. Couples no longer expect to have to give up time with each other to either extended family. They expect their spouse to be the source of enhanced well-being. This is true across all income levels and classes.[15]

Greedy, individualized marriages thus aid in undermining intergenerational relationships. Relationships between parents and adult children suffer from both the assumption of the nuclear family and the high expectations of marriage. Adult children do not spend as much time with parents or invest so heavily in their relationships as in the past because of the needs and expectations of marriage and the time and singular focus that it takes to sustain that relationship.

I will further argue in this book that marriage is not as greedy for women as it is for men. This is due to the greater consistency in the roles of wife/mother and daughter than in the roles of husband/father and son. If anything, women pull their husband in to their extended family, allowing them to maintain relationships with their parents, albeit not as close as prior to marriage. They do this, in part, because of the expectation that women will maintain close relationships with their parents throughout the life course.

The main purpose of this book, then, is to investigate how the transition to marriage differs for sons versus daughters, and in particular, how their relationship with their natal (i.e., birth) family changes after marriage. The book examines the quality of parent–adult child relationships following marriage and explores the *process* by which those relationships change. Underlying this examination is an investigation of just what it is about marriage that changes family relationships and how parent–adult child relationships differ for sons versus daughters. Particular emphasis is paid to cultural notions of marriage and cultural explanations for why marriage impedes (or improves) parent–adult child relationships, especially for sons.

The book is based on interviews with two subsamples: (1) mothers and (2) married men and women. It focuses on mothers' relationships with their adult children rather than fathers' because of mothers' kin-keeping role in the family and the closer relationships that adult children have with mothers as opposed to fathers.[16] Women express stronger obligations, are more likely to maintain family ties, and are most involved in assistance and caregiving within the family.[17] Mothers have more positive but not more negative relationships with their adult children than fathers. They also report higher quality relationships and more contact with at least one adult child than fathers.[18]

It was assumed, then, that mothers would be more cognizant of relationship changes and more involved in maintaining those relationships than fathers. However, mothers were also asked about their children's relationships with their father.

The second subsample consists of married men and women. In order to reduce any sampling bias, these adult children are not the adult children of the first subsample.[19] The sample includes those who were previously married and currently divorced to include a wide range of relationship effects. The married men and women were asked about their relationship with their father as well as their mother. The first and last names of all of the participants have been changed to protect confidentiality.

The results of this book have broader implications for understanding today's family. In particular, the results shed light on the recent discussion of just how nuclear or independent today's nuclear family is. It shows the extent to which intergenerational ties remain important today and the degree to which the nuclear family maintains broader connections. The book also illustrates the ways in which sons' and daughters' roles are changing. I argue that these changes are due both to men's more involved role as father and to the increased investment that parents have in their children's lives. The book informs us of how marriage transforms families and how the creation of a new and separate family is a significant life course event in the family life cycle that has been overlooked. Finally, it informs our understanding of today's individualized marriages and the meanings of those marriages for intergenerational ties. The book ends on a discussion of whether or not today's marriages can sustain such high expectations and the meaning of weakened intergenerational bonds for our aging population.

OUTLINE OF THE BOOK

Chapters 2 and 3 provide the background for the book. Chapter 2 includes five case studies of intergenerational relationships as an overview of and introduction to the complexities of parent–adult child bonds and to the importance of family context in understanding them. Chapter 3 examines the quality of mother–adult child relationships following marriage. It looks at both the range of experiences as well as typologies of relationships. In addition, it considers the factors that determine the quality of the relationship, including the effect of family context or family structure, which has not been sufficiently investigated to date. The effect of geographic distance on parent-child relationships is also examined. This important topic has not been adequately considered in recent years. One of the emerging themes from this chapter is the extent of intergenerational contact even when families live far away, despite the popular perception that the postmodern family has fallen apart and that the nuclear family has overshadowed intergenerational relationships.

Chapter 4 looks at the extent of contact, both visits and phone calls, between couples and their families following marriage. In particular, it considers whether couples see more of his family or her family after marriage. This is important in understanding whether and how men become incorporated into their wife's family. There is a popular perception that men "go to their wife's side of the family" once they marry, and this chapter investigates whether or not that is true. Included in this chapter is a discussion of the process by which men are pulled in to their wife's family and the ways in which men become more connected to their wife's family. This discussion leads to the broader question of whether and how families "lose" a son following marriage.

Chapter 5 investigates the extent to which the adage "A daughter is a daughter all of her life, but a son is a son 'til he takes him a wife" describes American families today. Do sons disengage from their families following marriage, and why? This chapter also includes a discussion of how (at least some) mothers are able to maintain close relationships with their sons following marriage. Underlying this is the question of whether men consider themselves as much a part of their natal family following marriage as women do and whether mothers expect and encourage their sons to be more independent of the family than daughters. This is a central component in uncovering just how parent–adult child relationships unfold over time and how expectations of sons versus daughters result in "son loss" in families.

Chapter 6 looks at the effect of marriage on intergenerational relationships and how it differs for sons versus daughters. It examines in greater detail how the relationship with the son changes after marriage and why daughters stay closer to the family following marriage than do sons. This chapter considers a number of factors, including the son's integration into his wife's family and the daughter-in-law's role as kin keeper.

Chapter 7 focuses on mothers and the challenges they face in maintaining intergenerational ties. This includes an investigation of how they handle the changes in their relationships with their sons following marriage and just what it is about the relationship between a mother and son that poses such a challenge when he marries. Included in the implications is a discussion of whether gender relationships within the family are changing.

Chapter 8 describes the development or evolution of parent–adult child relationships over time. It looks at both the effect of life course events in the children's and mother's lives as well as the passage of time. Given the focus of the book, it looks in particular at how the effects of marriage continue or subside over time. The impact of shared roles in adulthood and learned patterns of interaction on intergenerational relationships are discussed.

Chapter 9 considers the effects of both parental divorce and the adult child's divorce on intergenerational relationships. Included in the implications is a discussion of how the effect of divorce versus marriage on parent-child bonds differs by gender and what that tells us about the nature of ties with sons versus daughters.

Chapter 10 includes the advice that the mothers in the study offered to other parents. There were nine pieces of advice that fell within the following categories: allowing the couple to be independent, respecting the couple's marriage, being easy to get along with, creating a sense of family, and having alternative sources of identity in later life. The particular advice that is given is used to highlight mothers' understanding of how marriage affects relationships with adult children.

Chapter 11 investigates the reciprocal effects, that is, how intergenerational relationships impact marriage. Focusing on just the adult children in the study, it examines how both sons and daughters believe that their relationships with their own parents as well as their spouse's relationships with their parents have impacted their marriage. The implications of this chapter are particularly important given the continued high divorce rate in this country.

Chapter 12 summarizes the main findings and discusses what they tell us about the effect of marriage on intergenerational relationships, the process by which marriage changes those relationships, and how that differs by gender. It explains how mothers and adult children renegotiate their relationships following marriage and, based on the results, explores the nature and cultural meaning of marriage and relationships between mothers and adult children. The implications for older parents' reliance on their adult children are discussed, as is the "myth" of the nuclear family. The book ends by examining whether or not today's individualized marriages constitute a "greedy institution" and why.

The book also includes two appendixes. Appendix 1 describes the methodology. It includes a discussion of how respondents were recruited and how the sample was selected as well as a description of the sample. It also includes a description of the data analysis and defines the main variables used in the analysis. Appendix 2 gives the interview guidelines.

· 2 ·

Illustrations of
Intergenerational Relationships

$\mathcal{T}$he purpose of this chapter is to illustrate the nature of parent and adult child ties by providing five case studies of varied relationships. The intent of the chapter is to introduce the reader to the complexities of the relationships and to the importance of the overall family context in understanding the relationship before moving on to individual factors that affect parent and adult child ties. The case studies include large and small families as well as both those with and without intergenerational conflict.[1]

CASE STUDY ONE: THE COLES

Maggie Cole is seventy-four years old and widowed. She and her second husband are a working-class family. Maggie spent most of her adulthood as a stay-at-home mother. She had two children: Steven from her first marriage and Sarah from her second marriage. While Maggie and Sarah both describe their relationship with one another as being very close, they are both disappointed in their relationships with Steven. Sarah believes that Steven's distance is in part due to the fact that he was not her father's biological son. Maggie, however, said nothing to this effect. Both women believe that it was Steven's second marriage that greatly exacerbated the distance between them and Steven.

Maggie and Sarah have always been close. Sarah believes that they are now closer than they have ever been but that there was a period when the level of ambivalence was very high. She describes the changes in their relationship as follows:

When I was younger, probably for about fifteen years, I was really angry at my mother. I needed for her to be happy and to be there for me, but she couldn't. I was disappointed a lot, and I said things that I shouldn't have. At the same time, though, I was probably more connected to her than to anyone else in the world. We were *too* [her emphasis] intermeshed. . . . We are closer now. I don't *need* [her emphasis] my mother to be a certain way anymore, to be there for me. Her . . . limitations don't bother me anymore. I accept her for what she is, and we get along much better. It is like I am the parent now; I fill in where she is lacking. Since I don't get upset with her, I can take better care of her now that she is older.

Likewise, Maggie described their relationship as being "excellent" and the way that a mother and daughter relationship should be. She elaborated, "My daughter is the best thing that ever happened to me. Ever since I held that warm little body in my arms . . . well, she is the best thing I have ever done. She and my son. . . . No one can ever take that away from me. I am very proud of both of them. They have made something of themselves on their own."

While Maggie and Sarah describe their relationship with one another positively, they would both like to have closer ties with Steven. Sarah is also angry with Steven that he does not "do more" for their mother or show more of an interest in her. She feels that Steven purposefully remains distant and uninvolved.

In contrast to Sarah, Maggie did not express any anger toward Steven or toward what she saw as the causes of his distance. In fact, she did not express any disappointment in the first half of the interview at all. Once she became more comfortable, she said that she wished that they were closer and that he visited or called more often. She saw the change in Steven's behavior as occurring after his second marriage. She explained as follows:

My first daughter-in-law was like a second daughter to me. The three of us, we grew up together. I didn't think that they should get married so young, but they didn't listen. We are still close. Steven came around more then . . . every Sunday. Sometimes during the week too. . . . After the divorce, yes, he came around then too. . . . After his second marriage, he started staying away. My second daughter-in-law was very close to her people, and they did things with them. I just didn't feel comfortable with them. I think she was bored at our house . . . there wasn't as many of us, and we aren't as outgoing as they are. I didn't see as much of them as her family did. . . . No, there wasn't any conflict. We just didn't see them.

At the time of the interview, Steven was divorced for a second time and remarried. I asked Maggie if her relationship with her son had changed as a result of his third marriage. She explained, "No, I still don't see that much of him, and he doesn't call. I have to call him. Well, he comes a couple of times a year. I could be dead, though, and he wouldn't know it. I like his third wife, maybe because she is a nurse. She gets after him to call. . . . I think it is because he is a son. Sons just are not as close as daughters."

Sarah, on the other hand, was more critical of Steven than her mother was. She believed that Steven's distance was in part due to his second marriage, which set the stage for less contact. However, she also attributed his distance to the larger family context. She explained,

> My brother wasn't my father's biological son. None of us treated him any different. My father loved him like a son. But I think it affected his closeness to both me and my mother. . . . Sometimes I wonder if he blamed my mother . . . for not being able to work things out with his father. It was probably more, though, that he felt left out. That was his own doing though. . . . My brother is close to his wife and children, but that is it for family. . . . I wish that he and I were closer, but even more I wish that he could be closer to my mother for her sake. He really avoids being alone with my mom or talking about his feelings.

Maggie said that her husband's death had probably not affected her relationship with either of her children. Later she clarified by saying, "Well, it shouldn't have anyway." Sarah felt that her own relationship was affected in the short run, but not in the long run. She believed that it might have affected her brother's relationship with their mother over time. She stated, "Things were just more intense for all of us after my father died. He had kind of diluted things. Now it was just my mother, and us, and our spouses . . . although it really did not feel like our spouses made a difference. Maybe they did for my brother though."

While Sarah believed that her brother's second marriage had affected his relationship with the rest of the family, she further believed that his second divorce had impacted family relationships as well, especially for his children. She said,

> My brother's sons were never the type to call and say, "Hi Grammy, how are you?" Once their parents were divorced though, we saw them even less. They spent holidays with their mother and maternal grandparents, which is when we would have seen them. My brother did not do anything that would have encouraged them to stay in touch with their grandmother. He did not make sure that they saw her. Now that he is remarried, it is more of a blended family. We see more of his stepkids than his sons. It seems like our family always gets the short end of the stick.

Maggie said that her relationship with her own parents and her husband's relationship with his parents were always very close. She elaborated by adding, "We saw them or talked on the phone at least every other day. My kids saw them all of the time. They grew up being exposed to family and seeing us do for our parents. We were all together every Sunday. . . . I guess times have changed." Maggie added that she and her sister were not close while their children were growing up but that they are now that they are retired. She added, "[My sister] went through some rough times, but we are okay now."

CASE STUDY TWO: THE DELACROIX FAMILY

Miriam Delacroix was widowed and the mother of four children, two sons and two daughters. All of the children lived within a half-hour drive; one even lived on the same street as her mother. Miriam was well educated and had held a professional position since her youngest child entered school. She had been widowed for less than a year at the time of the interview. Miriam described herself as being Jewish by birth and upbringing but married to a Catholic. Miriam's two daughters were interviewed as well. Her sons, however, were not interested in being interviewed.

Miriam described her relationships with her children as all being very good. What was interesting though was how differently she described each relationship. Unlike the Cole family, where family history had played a large part in determining the relationships, it was differences in personalities that affected Miriam's relationships with her children. Her daughters also described different relationships with their mother and believed that their brothers' relationships were even more diverse. While all four of the children and their spouses and children saw one another frequently at family events, they did not see one another or call one another outside of the boundaries of those events. Interestingly, it was Miriam's oldest son and youngest daughter who had been closest despite the ten-year gap in their ages. Both of the daughters confirmed this. The younger daughter said that something had always "just clicked" between her and her older brother.

Miriam said that all of her children have been very caring and concerned since their father died. They have regular family get-togethers, and each of the children comes by frequently or calls to check on her. At several points throughout the interview, however, she emphasized that there were no "favorites" among her children.

Despite not having any favorites, Miriam stated that she was nearest to her older daughter, who lives on the same street as Miriam. She explained,

Joyce and I are extremely close. We talk two or three times a day. My sons are concerned for me. They always make sure that I am okay. But daughters express that concern more. I see more of them. . . . I am closer to Joyce than I am to Sylvia. Don't get me wrong. It [my relationship with Sylvia] is very close and warm, but she has a different personality than my older daughter, though. She holds more in. I see less of her than my older daughter. She is still busy with her kids. I go there every so often. I will stop by her house or she will stop by here. It is just not as close as Joyce.

Sylvia confirmed that her mother was closer to her sister Joyce than to her. But there did not appear to be any animosity or resentment. Miriam believed that she was closer to Joyce not only because she did not hold things in as much as Sylvia did but also because they were more alike. She added, "When I go to Joyce's house, I feel comfortable, at home. I can sit down and have coffee with her husband even if she is not there. Everything is in order and clean, like at my house. . . . There is a calm at Joyce's house which there isn't at Sylvia's. Joyce's kids have also been raised more like my own kids."

Sylvia pointed out that her troubled marriage was also affecting her relationship with her mother. Her mother and sister said nothing about this, however. Sylvia explained,

My house is very stressed. . . . My husband and I are not happily married. . . . My mother is very judgmental. She does not like him [my husband]. She and my father were super close. She does not understand that this is a very different generation . . . that couples can have problems. She has her own views. She doesn't make it any easier for me by giving her opinion all of the time. Plus, I don't want to have to be on edge all of the time while she is here. It is not fair to my husband either. He knows that she does not like him.

Sylvia was adamant, however, that her problems with her husband were not the result of her mother's dislike of him.

Miriam described her relationships with each of her sons as also being great. Both had lived away during college. She believes that their marriages had no effect on her relationships with them. Despite being very close to her younger son's wife, she stated that it did not affect her relationship with him. Miriam explained, "Nothing changed [when my younger son got married]. I have the best daughter-in-law in the world. She is a darling girl—very refined. She includes us in everything. If I don't want to join them, though, she understands. She is great. They got married right out of college." Miriam also pointed out that while her younger son doesn't call much, her daughter-in-law calls several times a week. Miriam said, "We don't necessarily talk about him or what he is doing. We have our own things to talk about, but at least I know that he is fine, and he knows that I am fine. If I needed anything, I would probably ask my daughter-in-law, though [versus my younger son]."

Miriam said that she is not as close to her older son's wife as she is to her second daughter-in-law, although she does care for her. However, she does not believe that this has made a difference in her relationship with her older son. She described both of her daughters-in-law as being "very good [daughters-in-law] because they did not pull her sons away, even though they are close to their own families." She also pointed out that she was very close to her sons-in-law, even though they were "independent." Miriam was proud of the fact that all of her children went out of their way to have warm relationships with their own in-laws. She felt that she had modeled that behavior for them. Joyce, however, felt that she and her husband were not particularly close to his parents.

Miriam believes that she was able to "cut the apron strings" with each of her children when they went off to college. She explained, "I could do that because I had a good marriage. It did not take away from anything [to let them go]."

Miriam and her daughters stated that all four of the children had been very close to their father. Her husband was an engineer, as is her oldest son. Her youngest son is a software engineer. She believes that both this shared interest and similar way of thinking about things made her sons closer to their father. She said, "They had a shared language, but also like minds. My sons don't say much and neither did my husband. . . . They don't take offense from one another for being that way because all three of them are alike." Similarly, Miriam's younger daughter, Sylvia, said that she was closer to her father than to her mother due to their similar personalities. She explained, "My dad and I were more alike. He wasn't judgmental. I could tell him anything. He didn't notice or care if the house was dirty. Plus, if he noticed, he would keep it to himself. I did not have to say much around him. We could just be together and not say anything. I miss that."

Thus, while the intergenerational relationships in Maggie Cole's family were affected by the history of the family and her son's marriage and divorce, the relationships in the Delacroix family were more affected by personality differences. The Delacroix siblings also illustrate how adult children can live near one another and have relationships that are free of conflict but still not feel close to one another. Again, this was due to perceptions, at least, of differences in personalities. The case of the Delacroix family also portrays how daughters-in-law can impact the mother-son relationship.

CASE STUDY THREE: THE GOLDSTEINS

Sixty-seven-year-old Sadie and her husband are the parents of three children who are all in their forties. Their daughter, Erica, lives only three blocks away, while their two sons, Jacob and Jonah, both live four hours away in opposite directions. Sadie and Isaac did not always live near Erica and her family, though. They moved to live near at least one of their children after retiring. It was Erica that they chose to be closest to.

Sadie described her relationship to Erica as follows:

> She is my pussycat. I get on her nerves and embarrass her, though. Our home is open to her children twenty-four hours a day. They can ride over on their bikes, but she does not abuse it. I go to all of the kids' school performances. I embarrass her sometimes. She is particularly wonderful. She is a very together person. I am in a wheelchair now, and she comes over and takes me shopping. She and the kids come over and take me out for a walk in the wheelchair, all of us. We are very generous to her. We would do anything she asks. Today we are taking her shoes to be repaired because she has a job interview [laughing].

Sadie, who laughs and makes jokes frequently, said that she expected that her children would always stay emotionally close and visit often, but she did not expect them to live physically nearby. After retiring, she said that she felt "down in the dumps" because she did not have any family nearby. She and Isaac then decided to move close to one of their three children. None of the children lived near one another. When asked why she decided to live near Erica, Sadie explained,

> My oldest son, Jacob, lived the closest to us at the time. He asked us to live near them. I thought about it. We would have still been four hours from the other two [children]. Jacob's in-laws already lived near them, though, and they were the primary in-laws. They tried to be equal and spend holidays with us too, but it wasn't really equal. They spent the holidays mostly with her family. Plus, they don't keep kosher, and that is an issue for us. I am a conservative Jew. . . . I would not raise the kids the way that his wife does. There is a lot of noise and clutter in their house. My granddaughter has very mild autism, and I can see that it bothers her. But they will go to a honky-tonk restaurant anyway. There is no brain there for me to explain it to, though [meaning that her daughter-in-law is brainless].

Sadie believes that she has a good relationship with Jacob. She attributes this to the fact that they both have a good sense of humor and can communicate through jokes as well as the fact that she can talk to him because he is quick like her. Sadie tries to avoid talking to Jacob's wife on the phone, however, because she is "chatty" and not as quick as Sadie would like her to be. Despite this, Sadie said, "She is sweet. She kisses me. She is a good girl." Sadie said that Jacob's marriage did not change her relationship with him because "he has always done what he wanted anyway."

Sadie would like to see more of Jacob and would like him to call her more often. Although there is no open conflict, barbed comments are exchanged between the two of them. For example, Sadie relayed the following incident.

> Keep in mind that I am a conservative Jew and keep kosher. Well, one day my granddaughter said to me, "I have had lobster, and I love lobster." I told her in front of Jacob, "You are not supposed to eat lobster. You are a Jew. . . ." People said to me, "You said that in front of Jacob?" He said to me, "It is your job to say what you need to say, and my job to do what I want."

Likewise, in describing her visits with Jacob's family, she said, "I went to visit last summer, and they were all so busy. I said to my son [laughing], 'You call this a visit? If I were dead, then you would have time for a visit. Why wait 'til then?'"

Although Sadie believes that she is free to "crash" at her son's home whenever she would like to, she does not visit more frequently than every ten weeks and then only for two or three nights. Sadie said that her husband does not like the trip and that after two days, Jacob's family "starts to get on her nerves until her blood pressure goes up."

Sadie's relationship with her younger son, Jonah, is even more complicated than her relationship with Jacob. She attributes this to the fact that she does not get along well with her daughter-in-law. Sadie explained, "I cannot even remember the name of the town that he lives in. That tells you a lot right there. . . . He married a very, very strange girl. She makes weird decisions in their life, and he goes along. My other daughter-in-law is chatty, but she is basically okay. This one, though, is cold and self-centered. I do not know why my son lets some things be." When asked to describe her relationship with Jonah, she stated, "For Mother's Day, they send me flowers. I would rather have a visit. I am not going to tell him that, though. If he cannot figure it out for himself. . . . We always spent three out of four Sundays with my parents, and the kids saw that. I have been invited only once to his kids' birthdays. If you move eight hours away, how can you expect to keep family ties?"

Unlike her relationship with her older son, Jacob, Sadie's relationship with Jonah was estranged by his marriage. According to Sadie, it was actually during the planning of the wedding that conflict surfaced. Sadie wanted

Jonah to have a traditional Jewish wedding, but her daughter-in-law wanted to eliminate many of the traditional customs. Sadie said that in the end, it was a kosher wedding even though her daughter-in-law did not like it. Sadie felt that her relationships with her son and grandchildren are further estranged by the "snobbish ways" that they have incorporated from her daughter-in-law and her very wealthy family.

At the end of the interview, Sadie's husband, Isaac, joined her and the interviewer. Sadie told him that she had explained "just how crazy their family was." At that point, the interviewer asked Isaac to describe his relationship with his children. Isaac said, "Well, whatever she said goes for me too. The only difference, though, is that I don't let it bother me. I figure that if someone wants to see me, that they can come to me. Or they can call me. If they don't, though, that is okay too." Sadie echoed, "Live and let live. Peace reigneth."

Unlike the other intergenerational relationships, Sadie's conversations with her sons were filled with barbed comments and arguing. Her relationships with both sons were negatively affected by the choices that they made to live outside of the conservative Jewish religion. Likewise, her relationship with her younger son was severely strained by her daughter-in-law. In sharp contrast, Sadie described her daughter in glowing terms and made no mention of her son-in-law. At one point, she said, "My daughter and her family . . . well, they can do no wrong." The Goldsteins confirm the tendency for parents to remain closer to daughters than sons over the life course.

CASE STUDY FOUR: THE BANES FAMILY

Like Maggie, Beth has two married children, including one son and one daughter. Beth is herself married and looking forward to retirement. She lives fifteen minutes away from her daughter and a half hour away from her son. At the time of the interview, Beth was eagerly anticipating her first grandchild.

When asked to describe her relationship with her daughter, Katelyn, Beth offered the following, "It is excellent. She was always a wonderful daughter. We were always very close. We are even closer now, especially since she has been pregnant. We do a lot of things together . . . shopping for baby clothes and things. She asks lots of questions now, asking for advice. She used to be a bit more standoffish than my son. She didn't tell me absolutely everything like my son did."

In some ways, Beth seemed to enjoy her son more than her daughter. When asked to describe her relationship with Thomas, she said,

It is very close. He is very outgoing. Very spontaneous, very open. He is just fun to be with, while my daughter is a little more reserved. He is easy to talk to and friendly. . . . We talk about whatever strikes his fancy. Now it is mostly about the house that he is building. He and his wife are living with us in the meantime, so I see him every day. . . . He asks for advice [about the house]. . . . He likes to shop, and I like to shop, so we do that.

However, when asked to compare the two relationships, Beth said that she was closer to her daughter because they are of the same sex. She said, "I can say more to her than Thomas. I can talk to her in more depth." This was surprising, since Beth seemed to be more intimate with her son than with her daughter.

Beth believed that her children's marriages had not changed either her or her husband's relationships with them. Beth said that her daughter-in-law included her in wedding plans from the start and has stayed involved in the family ever since. Beth said that she was worried that there might be tension between them once her son and daughter-in-law moved into her house, but there has not been. She pointed out, though, that they were not at home very often, since they both worked and spent their free time at the building site of their new home. Katelyn had been living with her fiancé for several years before she married. Beth felt that neither their living together nor their marriage had changed her relationship with Katelyn. She explained, "I still did some things with her and some things with [her and] her husband. She was probably closer to my husband than to me then. She confided in him more."

Interestingly, Beth believed that her relationship with each of her children was enhanced by their relationship with one another and with their father. Beth stated that her son and daughter have become much closer since her son got married. She explained, "Katelyn really likes [Thomas's wife]. It was Katelyn that really brought her into the heart of the family. The four of them get along so well and do a lot together. That makes it easier for us to be a close family. . . . It enhances our relationship with each of them." As for Beth's husband, she said, "Bill has always been great with the kids. He could always get through to Katelyn when I could not. She would come to ask him for advice, which benefited me. It helped my relationship with her that she was closer."

The Banes family thus exemplifies a situation where both parents maintain close ties with their children with no negative effect from their marriages. Beth, in fact, seems closer to her son Thomas than the vast majority of the mothers. What also makes the Banes family unique is the extent to which the children's close relationships with one another, as well as the sisters-in-law's close relationship, have improved intergenerational ties.

CASE STUDY FIVE: THE FERRANTE FAMILY

The Ferrante family is a typical working-class Italian family. Mary and her husband, Frank, have been married for over forty years and have three children. Her oldest son lives twenty-five minutes away, while her younger son and daughter each live within two miles of their parents' home. The Ferrantes see each of their children three to four times a week. On the days that they do not see one of them, they usually have a phone conversation.

Some might find the Ferrante's contact with their children to be too frequent and their lives to be too intermeshed. The Ferrante children call their parents whenever they need them, while the parents feel free to give advice at will. However, it should be pointed out that Frank and Mary were as close, and perhaps even closer, to their own parents. Frank and Mary spent their early years of marriage living on the second floor of Frank's parents' triple-decker, while Mary's parents lived one street over from theirs. Their own children were constantly in and out of their grandparents' homes. To Frank and Mary, then, the degree of contact with their children is not unusual.

Mary described her relationship with each of her children as being very close. She said that she feels a little closer to her daughter because she is another woman, but that this does not take away anything from her relationship with her sons. In fact, she is so close to her older son that he has shared his sexual performance problems with his mother. Mary said that it made her very uncomfortable to hear about it, but she was pleased that he felt comfortable talking about it with her. Mary also meets her oldest son frequently for lunch because he works nearby. Mary said that Tom also calls her whenever he cooks, which is frequent, to find out what spices she uses and if he is "doing things correctly."

Mary and all three of her children typically spend large segments of the evening and weekends helping one another out with home repairs, shopping, and spending time together. Mary said that they also sometimes go away for the weekend together, with their children's in-laws as well. Mary said that she does not think she has ever gone an entire week without seeing one of her children, except when they first moved out of the family home and into their own apartments. She said, "That was when they needed the most independence, and I let them have it." Mary also cares for her daughter's only child. She explained the onset of that arrangement as follows,

> When my daughter had her son, she planned to go back to work after three months. I was hoping that she wouldn't do it. . . . She and her husband planned to put him in day care. I told my daughter that she was not going to put my grandson in day care, over my dead body. I told her that he

would be better off with his grandma than in any day care center and that I was *not* [her emphasis] going to let her do that. She let him come and stay with me and it was the best thing for him too.

Other than instances like this, Mary feels that conflict with any of her three children is infrequent and short-lived.

Mary also has very good relationships with both of her daughters-in-law and her son-in-law. She made a point of stating that her older son's wife was previously married and has three children from that marriage. Mary added, "People sometimes say that Shelly came with baggage. I don't feel that way. I feel that she was a gift and children are bonuses. I will take grandchildren any way that I can get them." Mary is also very proud of the fact that she and Frank paid for her older son's wedding. They were going to have a backyard wedding, but Mary said "she wanted to do it right." She added, "That way we could have a say about what was happening too."

Mary and Frank are also close to their second daughter-in-law. Liz's parents live in Florida, so Liz and Mary's son Tony fly there for Christmas. Mary said that it did not bother her, though, because they stayed for Christmas Eve. She said that it was also a benefit to have the other grandparents in Florida so that she could be the "primary grandmother" for the grandchildren when they came along.

Mary and Frank did not always get along with their son-in-law, however. She explained,

When [my daughter] brought him home, I was furious. First of all, he was eight years older than her. When I asked how she met him, she said that it was at an A.A. meeting. I almost froze, and then I hit the roof. I said, "You know how grandma and grandpa were. You have heard my stories. Why would you go and get involved with someone like that? What were you *thinking* [her emphasis]?" She said, "Ma, I said recovering alcoholic. He doesn't drink anymore." Then we got to know him, and he doesn't drink. He treats her like a princess. We love him now.

In sum, Mary and Frank were able to maintain very close relationships with their three adult children and children-in-law despite, or perhaps because of, their intermeshed lives with each. Marriage did little to change their relationships with their adult children. If anything, the family and the extent of love within it just grew larger.

The purpose of this chapter was to set the stage for further analysis by providing the reader with an in-depth look at five distinct families. The five

families that were chosen were intended to offer an array of family types and relationships. They were not necessarily intended to be representative, however. These examples highlight the impact of the overall family context and the need to consider the effects of the extended family when studying parent–adult child relationships. In the next chapter we will look at the effect of specific factors in determining the quality of those relationships and how they change following marriage.

· 3 ·

Relationships between Parents and Adult Children

*R*elationships between parents and their adult children are among the most significant ties within the family. Parent-child relationships are generally positive with typically relative proximity, frequent contact, and emotional closeness.[1] Among those parents who do not co-reside with a child, approximately three-quarters live within a thirty-five-minute drive of at least one child, and half have two children within this range.[2] Nearly 80 percent report weekly contact with at least one child. Shared affection is one of the cornerstones of intergenerational relationships. The most common relationships are referred to as "tight knit" or "sociable" and are characterized by high levels of affection and the opportunity to see one another. "Tight-knit" relationships also include an exchange of resources, typically flowing from parents to children earlier in life.[3] Parents tend to report more positive relationships than their children, particularly on measures of closeness.[4]

However, parent–adult child relationships are not all positive. Despite the high degree of affection, conflict is often present as well. This situation, together with the presence of both positive and negative feelings toward the other person, is referred to as ambivalence and is fairly frequent in parent–adult child relationships. Interestingly, ambivalence is greater the closer the family relationship.[5] As a result, mothers feel more ambivalence than fathers.[6] Families are also more likely to experience "collective ambivalence" when there are multiple children in the family.[7] Ambivalence is often manifested during status transitions experienced by both adult children and their parents.[8] This would suggest that marriage might be a time in which difficulties arise in the relationship.

23

Obligation and exchange are the additional cornerstones of inter-generational relationships. In fact, obligations to one's own parents and children rank the highest of all personal relationships.[9] In a recent study of adult children, 40 to 50 percent of the children stated that there is a family obligation to assist an older parent.[10] While exchange of emotional support and companionship are frequent, exchanges of practical assistance are more rare.[11] Parents and adult children exchange different resources. The flow of financial aid and services tends to be from parents to children only. In contrast, parents seek companionship, affection, and finally caregiving from their children. However, because parent-child relationships are embedded within a highly gendered family network, the wife's parents tend to provide and receive more assistance than the husband's parents.[12] Although both men and women report higher affective closeness to their own parents than in-laws, the difference is greater for women than men.[13] Men have more contact with their in-laws than with their own kin, while the opposite is true for women.[14] This would imply that couples also see more of her family than his. The process of men being pulled in to their wife's family is discussed in chapter 4.

Despite the norms of obligation and assistance across generations, norms of independence are also widely upheld. When adult children assist their parents, they try to maintain their parents' independence as much as possible, referred to as "the principle of least involvement."[15] Likewise, adult children are expected to be responsible for their own well-being. According to previous researchers, nuclear families are assumed to be independent of the wider kin network, and "outsiders" are expected to protect the privacy of the nuclear family.[16] This book challenges that notion. Instead, it is argued that mothers, in particular, cultivate and expect continued involvement of their adult children, and often their spouses, within the extended family.

Distant living is also common for parents and adult children, as children move away to take advantage of job and educational opportunities, and parents move away following retirement. The typical distant child visits twice a year. While only 10 percent visit less than once a year, one-third visit three times a year or more. Average visits last for four days but range from one day to six weeks.[17] An increase in distance leads to improved relationships between both parents and adult children in most instances, but it leads to a decline in the relationship between mothers and sons. While daughters do not need frequent physical contact to maintain a relationship, sons do because they take less initiative in maintaining kin relationships.[18] This book argues that relationships with adult sons also worsen following marriage because of men's lesser involvement in kin networks.

SONS' RELATIONSHIPS WITH PARENTS

Although there was some diversity in sons' relationships with their parents, the diversity was not as great as that reported for an earlier study of in-law relationships.[19] This suggests that close family relationships, parent-child versus in-law, tend to be more homogeneous than heterogeneous. In general, sons had a "tight-knit" relationship with at least one of their parents from the perspective of both mothers and adult men. These relationships are high in affection, opportunities to see one another, and an exchange of resources.[20] However, relationships typically included some sort of complication or nuance, so that they were not necessarily perfect. Also, relationships with mothers, versus fathers, were often quite different. For example, both Chris and Ed had "tight-knit" relationships with their mothers but not with their fathers, who had abused either them or their mothers. Chris rarely saw his father and felt no affection for him, while Ed saw his father often at family events but felt little or no affection. Ed said that he acted the part of the dutiful son to keep up appearances for his father's sake. Ed saw his mother several times a week, while Chris saw his mother several times a month but talked to her on the phone daily. Both men had been involved in caregiving for their mothers over the last few years. While Ed was the sole caregiver for his mother, Chris had a sister who provided the hands-on care. Ed even provided housing for his mother among the several properties that he owned.

Ethan and Mike had "tight-knit" relationships with both of their parents. However, their relationships with their mothers had become strained over the years due to conflict between their wives and mothers. Ethan felt "pulled" between his mother, who wanted to see him more, and his wife, who wanted to limit visits with his parents. He prioritized his wife's wishes because, according to him, he had a "contract" with her that included negotiating differences, while he had no such contract with his mother. Ethan recognized that his relationship with his mother was strained by the situation, however, and that his mother was frustrated that she did not see him more. Ethan said that when they did visit, he had to be on his guard always to make sure that his mother did not "intrude" on his and his wife's privacy or determine the way that they spent their time during the visit. Yet Ethan felt that he and his mother shared political and social outlooks, which was important to him. Mike's wife had an even worse relationship with his mother. While Mike and his mother had always been very close, he now felt a significant estrangement from both her and his siblings. Although Mike kept in touch with them, it was not how it had been before he married. Mike felt that his mother and sister were unfairly critical of his wife because, according to them, she "came from the wrong side of the tracks." Mike said that their response to both her and his son was embarrassing and disappointing to him. On the other hand, seeing his mother "for what she was" had made Mike much closer to his father. Mike said that his father had always been the "black sheep" of the family since the divorce. But Mike and his father have become the best of friends since Mike married. In fact, it was the conflict between his wife and mother that brought them together; Mike sought the advice of his father when problems erupted between his wife and mother.

All of the above sons exchanged instrumental support with their parents, although the extent of support varied. Some also shared financial support. With the exception of Ed, most of this support was from parent to son. Instrumental support included babysitting, regular assistance with yard work and home repair, ironing, sharing of resources, and financial overseeing. Mothers also frequently reported instrumental support from their sons. One of the mothers stated, "My [oldest] son was always the one who took care of everything for me. My husband traveled . . . and he wasn't ever really handy anyway. My son would drop anything though when I called him . . . until his wife got him to move. That changed everything for our family."

Samuel and Tim both had "sociable" relationships with their mothers. They expressed affection toward their mothers and regularly visited. However, neither of the men exchanged resources with their mothers. Both Samuel and his mother were relatively poor and had very little that they could exchange beyond affection. Tim and his mother exchanged assistance every now and then. Tim sometimes fixed things in his mother's house, while she occasionally babysat for his daughters. There was very little beyond this limited reciprocity, though. Tim's relationship with his mother was not strained by anything, but he had had to "referee" conflict between his wife and mother over the years, particularly around visiting during the holidays. However, he hoped that after several years of marriage "all of the kinks" in the system of visiting had been worked out. He pointed out that the equitable pattern of visiting that they had established was highly dependent on other extended family members on both sides of the family maintaining the agreed-upon schedule for the holidays.

Colin was the only son who felt affection for his parents but had little contact or exchange with them. Colin regularly stopped to visit his parents while he worked but did not share holidays with them because, according to Colin, his wife could not get along with her parents or his parents. Colin was very frustrated by this and had once separated from his wife due to her "isolation" (as he referred to it). Colin said that he liked having people around and that he wanted to see more of his parents. At the time of the interview, though, his contact was limited to stopping in for coffee with his parents.

Colin explained, "When we got back together, she agreed that we would see more of my parents. She has not kept up her end of things, though . . . the priest even heard her. . . . I just don't know what to do anymore, though . . . how much longer I can stay married like this."

Only Robert had a "detached" relationship with both of his parents with low levels of affection, exchange, and contact. Robert said that he and his parents were once quite close. However, shortly after he married he learned of an inappropriate incident within his family that his parents had overlooked. Since then, Robert has had no contact with his parents. He said that he has no regrets about this. While his parents continue to try to see him, he does not respond. Robert, however, continues to see his siblings annually.

DAUGHTERS' RELATIONSHIPS WITH PARENTS

The daughters' relationships with their parents ran the gamut from "tight knit" (characterized by high affection, opportunities to see one another, and a functional exchange of resources) to "detached" relationships (which included little affection, opportunity to see one another, or exchange of resources). Unlike the sons, many of the daughters had "obligatory" relationships with their parents, characterized by low affinity but high opportunities to see one another and high exchange of resources. In fact, the most common relationships with parents for women included "tight-knit" or "obligatory" relationships. Daughters are more likely to remain close to parents, even when affection for parents is low. Rarely did daughters have "intimate but distant" relationships where there was little opportunity to see one another or exchange of resources. This included daughters who had always lived far from their parents due to their husband's work as well as those who lived as little as two hours away. For example, Ruth called her mother several times a day but did not see her or exchange resources due to both women's poverty-level standard of living despite living only two hours apart. The relationship was also affected by the mother's alcoholism and Ruth's disappointment in the limited affection that her mother gave to her. Only one daughter had a "detached" relationship. Kathy kept her distance from her mother due to her embarrassment over being divorced and fear of her mother's judgment against her.

Interestingly, daughters were more likely to have "tight-knit" relationships over "sociable" relationships than sons. This confirms earlier findings that couples are more likely to exchange resources with the wife's parents than with the husband's parents.[21] There were also daughters who had high affinity with their parents and exchanged resources but who did not have frequent opportunities to see their parents. Their relationships with their parents were more like the "tight-knit" than the "intimate but distant" relationships. This categorization, however, is missing from typologies of parent–adult child relationships.[22]

Like the sons, several of the daughters characterized their relationship with their mother differently than their relationship with their father. It was more common for daughters to say that they were closer to their mother than their father. However, a few of the daughters said that they were closer to their father because their father was more easygoing or less judgmental than their mother. These daughters still described their relationship with their mother in positive terms, but they were just closer to their father. Several of the daughters whose parents were divorced said that their stepmother strained their relationship with their father. One of the daughters, for example, said that her stepmother tried to keep her away from her father and did not allow her to visit. Another daughter said that her stepmother told her father to stop helping her because she should learn to rely on her own husband.

Despite the fact that daughters described their relationships with parents as being overall positive, there was still some conflict in all but a few of the relationships. That is, most of the daughters described ambivalent relationships. Several of the daughters stated that they had a "dysfunctional" relationship with their mother. Amber, for example, stated the following, "My mom and I are very close . . . but I play the mother role. I mind it, but I have accepted it. Like right now there is conflict because my mother is trying to get a married man to leave his wife for her. I am against it, and I am trying to make my mother see that it is wrong." A more common complaint among daughters was that their mother was judgmental or did not respect their independence enough, despite their being very close to their mother. Vicki described a very overbearing mother who expected her daughter to be constantly at her side and who was quite judgmental. According to Vicki, her mother felt that she did not make enough money and that her husband was "not good enough for her." Another daughter was the caregiver for her mother, but there was a thread of animosity toward her mother because she had not supported her decision to go to school earlier in life. Dawn explained,

> My mother and I were always close . . . maybe too close. I was the only daughter, and my father died early. . . . My mother was sick a lot and was in a state of need. . . . There was conflict surrounding my going to school. She did not want me to go because I would not be able to help her enough, but my education was important. I went anyway but I went nearby so that I could come home on weekends to help my mother. . . . I did not go out with the others [friends] on Friday night to help her. . . . I did not go to Seattle when I had a chance. I was resentful of all that I had to do.

THE EFFECT OF FAMILY CONTEXT

Family context affected relationships between parents and adult children in a number of ways. The size of the family had a significant effect, especially for daughters. Daughters who had one or more sisters, in particular, were less likely to describe "tight-knit" relationships. These daughters stated that their mother was closer to their other daughters or sons. Likewise, mothers typically described their relationships as being closer to one of their children than to the others when they had more children. They felt closer to children who were more like them (i.e., they either had similar personalities or interests) or whom they described as being "more open." In smaller families, though, both mothers and children were more likely to describe relationships in terms of "tight-knit" characteristics.

Adult children whose siblings were unavailable were also more likely to describe "tight-knit" relationships. This included adult children whose siblings lived far away as well as children whose siblings did not get along with their parents or who had distanced themselves from their parents. For example, one of the daughters said that she was closer to her mother and did more for her because her brother did less. She said that her mother had been hurt by her brother's (emotional) distance, which endeared her mother to her even more.

A mother's absence during her child's adolescence also had a significant impact on parent–adult child relationships. One of the mothers explained her daughter's emotional distance as being the result of her own need to work while her daughter was young and her resulting reliance on her daughter to care for her younger brother. Frannie stated,

> Our relationship is not what it should be. . . . It is not as close as I would like. She had a lot of responsibility while she was growing up. I was separated for awhile. I guess it took its toll on her. . . . I wrote her a letter last month and told her that I would like to be closer. I don't see her as often as I would like, just holidays. . . . I think that she would have liked me to have been home more while she was growing up. We lived with my mother in between my two marriages, and she was more like the mother.

Frannie and her daughter saw one another only on holidays and birthdays despite the fact that they lived in the same town. Likewise, another daughter, Dawn, said that although she felt close to her mother, there was some distance between them because she was actually raised by her aunt during her "formative" years when her mother was ill. She explained, "It was hard. My mother wasn't there for the important formative years, like when I started my

period. She was busy with my younger brother, and I was always independent. So that bond wasn't established. . . . My mother's sister is like a mother
to me too. She was the person that took us in for four years. She was the one
who was there for the formative years." Despite this distance, though, Dawn
was the primary caregiver for her mother.

Parental divorce also affected intergenerational relationships. This topic
is discussed separately and in detail in chapter 9 along with a discussion of the
impact of the adult child's divorce on intergenerational ties.

GEOGRAPHICALLY DISTANT RELATIONSHIPS

Nearly one-third of the adult children lived one hour or more away from at
least one parent. Interestingly, the sons were more likely to live a long distance
away than the daughters. Among the daughters who lived far away, only one
had what would have been defined as a "tight-knit" relationship with both
parents had she lived closer. In fact, Katie was making plans to move closer to
her parents. She had originally left the area for job opportunities but wanted
to move back now that she had a young daughter. Ruth and Amy, however,
were more typical distant children in that they had "detached" relationships
with their parents. It did not seem that the distance caused the estrangement,
however. Rather, it was just the opposite. They had deliberately moved away
in order to see less of their parents. Only Elizabeth's relationship lacked affinity due, at least in part, to the distance. However, Elizabeth also pointed
out that her parents had always been reserved and that there was "no reason"
for her and her husband not to move around the country. Thus, it would appear that living at a distance is related to worse relationships with parents for
daughters than for sons.

Sons were more likely to have good relationships with their distant
parents. Both Samuel and Ethan had maintained positive relationships with
their parents over the years despite significant distance. Both visited with
parents several times a year and felt that the distance did not inhibit their
relationships. Samuel said that he would like to see his family more but he
could not afford the cost of transportation. Ethan would have been willing to
see more of his parents but his wife did not want to see them as often. They
compromised on the frequency and location of visits.

Slightly more than one-third of the mothers had at least one child who
lived one or more hours away. Mothers were more likely than adult children
to say that the distance affected parent-child relationships. Also typical, one
mother said that the distance affected her relationship with her son but not

with her daughter. Her daughter stayed emotionally close and visited often despite the physical distance, while her relationship with her son was more constrained and remote after he moved. These mothers said that they felt closer to their geographically proximate children.

Those mothers who were most unhappy with their child's distant living were distressed by the lack of time that they had together. What made this worse was that when they did visit their children, their sons or daughters were usually working or absorbed in their own activities. For example, Sadie said, "We visit . . . more like every ten weeks. I can always crash there whenever I want, though. The last time that I went, they were all busy all of the time. I said to [my son], 'Is this called a visit?' . . . We stay for two or three nights until my blood pressure goes up." Likewise, busy work schedules prevented children from visiting their parents more often. Sandra explained, "My son came out for a wedding last summer and he was on the computer the whole time. I thought about switching the circuit breakers to get his attention. He is a workaholic. . . . Even when I see him, I don't see him because he is on the computer. . . . I would like him to visit more, but he doesn't like to leave work."

A few of the mothers had been against their children living so far away. The others saw it as an expected part of pursuing their careers, but did not see it as related to marriage. One mother went further and said that she encouraged her children to move away and live independently. Sally felt that her children had their own separate families and that she and her husband were not a part of those families, despite having warm and loving relationships.

One of the mothers believed that her child's distance actually improved their relationship. Camilla and her husband used to visit her daughter and spouse regularly despite the fact that they lived 1,200 miles away. The couples even vacationed together, along with her daughter's in-laws. Camilla's daughter is remarried now, though, and Camilla feels very uncomfortable around her new son-in-law. She stated, "Now it is probably good that [she] is so far away . . . because of the husband. I don't go there as often or stay as often because I . . . just find him odd. . . . My daughter still comes here for around five weeks every summer. . . . It is probably best this way."

Sadie was the only mother who had moved to be closer to one of her children. She said that she did so because she was starting to feel somewhat depressed by having her children so far away during her retirement. One of her sons and her daughter both wanted her to move closer to them. She decided to live closer to her daughter because, as she put it, the "primary grandmother" (i.e., the wife's mother) already lived near her son and his family. Sadie hoped that her sons would eventually move closer to her. Each one lived four hours away, but in opposite directions.

THE VAST EXTENT OF CONTACT

One of the surprising findings of this study was the vast extent of contact between parents and their adult children. Many of the mothers and children called one another four or five times a day and visited several times a week. Some visited as often as every day. Even those who lived at a distance saw one another as frequently as six or seven times a year for one or more weeks each visit. Children tended to visit for shorter periods due to their work. Camilla's daughter spent five weeks with her each summer, leaving her spouse and home in Florida.

Most of the parents and adult children who lived in the same vicinity saw one another at least twice a month. More often, it was several times a week. Visits included spending time together on holidays, stopping by for coffee or to see the grandchildren, providing instrumental support, or dropping off exchanged resources. Interestingly, the extent to which (geographically proximate) parents and adult children saw one another did not vary by class.

SUMMARY AND IMPLICATIONS

While relationships between adult daughters and their parents run the gamut from being extremely close to estranged with every type in between, there is less diversity in the relationships between adult sons and their parents. For example, daughters are more likely than sons to have an "obligatory" relationship with their parents. That is, daughters will see their parents and exchange resources even when there is little affection in the relationship. This finding will be born out again and again in this book and confirm the first part of the adage that "a daughter is a daughter all of her life," no matter what the circumstances. In contrast, sons will distance themselves or detach from the relationship when affection is low. As a result, a higher percentage of sons had "detached" relationships than daughters in this study. Daughters were also more likely to have a "tight-knit" relationship than a "sociable" one in comparison to sons. This is consistent with earlier findings that couples are more likely to exchange resources with the wife's parents than the husband's parents.[23]

Although sons frequently had a "tight-knit" relationship with at least one of their parents, their relationship with their parents was more affected by their spouse than were the daughters' relationship with parents. This was according to both sons and mothers. In particular, sons were less likely to see their parents if their spouse did not get along with them. In contrast, there appeared to be less conflict between in-laws and husbands, or it at least had less effect on the daughter's/wife's relationship with her parents. Husbands may be more accepting of their in-laws or have an easier time getting along with them because they are pulled in to their wife's family. They may also be more willing to get along because of the assumed closeness between daughters and their parents. I will also argue that men have an easier time getting along with their in-laws because relationships are less important to their identity. As a result, it is less likely that there will be disappointments in the relationship or aspects of the relationship that keep them away.

Not surprisingly, sons are more likely to live a long distance away than are daughters. Yet, distant living was related to poorer relationships with parents for daughters but not for sons. This is in contrast to earlier suggestions that distance presents more of an obstacle to maintaining a close mother-son relationship because sons take less initiative in kin relationships.[24] It is more likely that this is a selection effect, however. That is, those daughters that did live a long distance had strained relationships with parents even before they moved. These findings also suggest that having a close relationship with a parent inhibits distant living for daughters but not sons. In fact, the one parent who did move to be closer to a child chose to live near her daughter over her son, even though her son had asked her to live nearby as well. Again, we see evidence of the close relationship between parents and their adult daughters, lending support for the adage that "a daughter is a daughter all of her life." Sons may also be better able to maintain a positive relationship with distant parents because there is less expectation of the relationship in general.

Ambivalence was more common among daughters than among sons. This was likely due to two factors. Sons that experience negative feelings are more likely to stay away and thus experience "detached" relationships. In contrast, daughters feel greater obligation to stay in touch and cultivate a relationship even when there are problems in the relationship. In addition, sons with good relationships are less likely to note problems because relationships in general are less of a focus for men. In the next chapters we will look to see whether or not daughters (and their spouses) still have more contact with parents despite the existence of this ambivalence, and why.

We began the chapter by asking the question of whether or not intergenerational ambivalence is manifested by status transitions, such as marriage. Conflict between spouses and parents certainly created ambivalence for a number of sons and, to a lesser extent, for a few daughters as well, even though sons described less ambivalence overall. Those sons whose wife did not get along with their parents felt pulled between their wife and parents. They realized that they disappointed their parents by not visiting more. Mothers also expressed disappointment when their sons decreased visiting after marriage. Sons attempted negotiating with both parties, but it was their relationship with their parents that was more impacted. Yes, ambivalence is manifested by status transitions. Even when there is ambivalence to begin with, the complexities of that ambivalence multiply following marriage and the incorporation of an in-law into the family. In the concluding chapter, we will discuss the implications and what can be done to minimize the ambivalence.

Family context played an important role in determining the quality of intergenerational relationships. Most noteworthy, adult children were less likely to describe "tight-knit" relationships when there were several siblings available to the mother. Indeed, mothers also described relationships as being closer to one child than another. Clearly, the characteristics of a relationship with one child affect relationships with other children; in unraveling the complexities of intergenerational relationships, the family as a whole needs to be understood as a system. "Collective complexity" needs to be incorporated both in theory and in research on relationships between parents and adult children.

This chapter looked at the quality of relationships between parents and adult children who are currently married or divorced. Overall, relationships are better than was predicted, with strong evidence for daughters' close relationships with their parents. Later in the book we will examine how marriage changed those relationships and whether or not there is evidence of marriage being a greedy institution that undermines intergenerational relationships. In the next chapter we will examine differences in patterns of contact that couples have with the wife's family versus the husband's and the implications for relationships between mothers-in-law and daughters-in-law.

• *4* •

Gender Differences in
Contact with Parents and In-Laws

Do Couples See More of Her Family Than His?

*P*revious research has shown that gender plays a central mediating role in studies of intergenerational relationships.[1] In particular, female members of the family are more involved than male members in maintaining intergenerational relationships across adulthood.[2] The level of contact is even greater when both members are women. That is, mothers and daughters have more frequent contact than both fathers and sons and mixed-gender relationships.[3] Parents both visit and talk on the phone more with daughters than with sons.[4] The effect is also cumulative. Parents with at least one daughter report more frequent contact than do parents with only sons, but the frequency of contact increases the more daughters the parent has.[5]

Gender also mediates interaction between married individuals and their parents and parents-in-law. In particular, married women have more visits and phone contact with their parents than do married men, and men talk on the phone with their in-laws more than women. While women are more likely to contact and help their own parents versus their in-laws, there are no such patterns for men.[6] As a result, it seems that men and women have more contact with the wife's parents than with the husband's parents. This is consistent with additional findings that couples are more responsive to the needs of the wife's parents and are less likely to exclude her parents from care when both sets of parents need assistance.[7] However, couples do try to be "fair" in the distribution of assistance when both sets of parents are alive.[8]

One might expect women to have more contact with both their parents and their parents-in-law due to their kin-keeping role. However, women's more central role in intergenerational relations appears to be restricted to their natal family and does not include their in-laws. Overall, both men and women feel stronger obligation and more affective closeness toward their parents than their in-laws,[9] but the difference is greater for women than for men.[10] There is also greater ambivalence toward in-laws compared to parents for women than men.[11] Relationships with parents are paramount and close to the top of the hierarchy of obligations for women, while the same does not hold true for men. Sociologists Alice Rossi and Peter Rossi hypothesized that women's closer ties with their parents would draw their husbands in to closer ties with his parents-in-law than parents.[12] Other researchers' findings would appear to support this hypothesis. However, the authors point to the need to explain the process by which this occurs after marriage. In particular, they suggest that future researchers ask how these intergenerational relations are transformed with the transition to marriage.[13]

The purpose of this chapter is to answer these questions. The chapter begins by examining whether couples visit the wife's parents versus the husband's parents more (as well as confirming whether men and women call their own parents versus their in-laws more). Earlier research suggests that women see more of their own parents than in-laws, while husbands do not, and that men call their in-laws more than their parents, while women do not.[14] However, we do not know whether the *couple* sees more of her parents than his. Knowing this is important in uncovering the process by which men get drawn in to their wife's kin network. Second, the chapter examines *why* adult children have more contact with one side of the family versus the other. It considers the reasons that women are more likely to contact and help their own parents than their in-laws relative to men as well as the context in which women might get drawn in to their husband's kin network. Third, the chapter examines the *process* by which men get pulled in to their wife's kin network after marriage and the ways in which men are more connected to the wife's family.

Public discourse implies that families "lose" their sons following marriage. The next chapter examines to what extent this perception holds true and why. I argue that myths of losing one's son following marriage are based more on a decrease in contact rather than experiencing any qualitative difference in the relationship. Couples spend more time with the wife's parents than the husband's parents because of an expectation of continued closeness with daughters. Daughters, who organize family visits and holidays, maintain closer contact with their own kin out of familiarity, and husbands comply and participate more in her family. Decreased contact with the son contributes to strained relationships within the family, particularly between the mother-in-law and daughter-in-law and a mother's sense of having "lost" her son.

VISITS WITH PARENTS AND IN-LAWS

There is a slightly greater likelihood of couples seeing more of the wife's relatives than the husband's relatives than vice versa. However, the differences are not as large as was predicted by available studies. Less frequent was the tendency for a couple to see both sides equally. Many of the couples said that they tried to be equal but tended to favor the wife's side of the family.

It was predicted that a large number of the couples would see more of the wife's family than the husband's family. However, there were many reasons why couples saw more of the husband's family than the wife's family. For example, several couples lived closer to the husband's family than to the wife's family. In these instances, the couple had *chosen* to live closer to his than her family when they were first married, suggesting the wife's willingness to put his family first. Joy explained, "We moved closer to [my husband's] family when I finished school because his mother wasn't working and they [his family] are really close. They really wanted us to be nearby. My family . . . well there are lots of us, so it didn't matter so much."

Although it was more common for a couple to see more of the parents that lived nearby, this was not always the case. According to one wife, it was the *greater* distance to her husband's family that resulted in seeing more of them than her family. Because it took longer to drive to her husband's family, they often tended to stay for three or four days rather than the three or four hours that they spent with her family that lived one hour away. As a result, they saw more of his family overall. Sophie noted the following, however: "We actually argue about this, who we spend more time with. We are both protective of making sure that we see our parents equally, that they are treated equally . . . but then when we are there they drive us crazy and we wonder why we went."

Couples also saw more of the husband's family when there was some estrangement or problem between the wife and her family. One of the wives had "nothing to do with her family" according to her husband, Pete. He, however, did like to have his family around, so he would take the initiative to invite them to visit. Still, they spent a limited amount of time with Pete's family because his wife, Mary, did not get along with his family either. Pete was very distressed by this. He explained,

> Now we spend the holidays with just our family because it is so stressful to be with my parents. My wife does not get along with them. We see them just minimally, but we don't see hers at all. . . . Before we were married, she *did* get along with them [his parents]. She even lived with them for a year to save money. . . . After the wedding, everything changed. . . . We

separated for awhile. . . . When we got back together, I told her, "Look, things have to be different, beginning with my parents." She said that she understood, but I tell ya, any little thing offends her.

Deb stated that her family was not close or openly affectionate, so she preferred to spend time with her husband's family, which was very close. Cindy said that she spends more time with her husband's family than her own because her family did not allow her husband to visit due to his skin color (i.e., race). Other wives also explained that there were problems with their family that made them keep their distance, but they did not have problems with their husband's family.

One of the husbands, Ed, pointed out that whom they spent time with had varied across the life course. His family included five generations when they were first married, and there were many family events to attend. At that time, his wife, Sue, was anxious to get away from her family, where there was too much drinking. She explained,

> I had a feeling of family when I was a little kid. Then, when I was a teenager, I looked and saw what they were. They were always drinking and sniping at each other. I could not wait to get away from them . . . so I left when I was nineteen and moved in with Ed. I just stayed away from them. . . . I was closer to Ed's family. I liked how they took care of all of the women.

They spent more time with Sue's family later when their children were growing up. Her family provided many activities at their home for the couple's sons. More recently, though, Ed and Sue have gone back to spending more time with his family because of a rift between Ed and his in-laws over a business matter involving both couples. Sue also sees much less of her parents because of the problems between them and her husband. She explained,

> I used to take the kids to visit them a lot. They had a pool, and I could take the boys swimming. We could drop in anytime and see them. We would spend half a day together or have a cookout. We were together a lot. Now I just go over every now and then so they can see the kids. I don't go like I used to. When I am there, we don't really talk much. I try to have my brothers and sisters there.

A minority of the women said that their husband saw his parents infrequently. Usually the wife urged the husband to visit more for his parents' sake. The wives explained that there was not a problem necessarily between their husband and his parents but that their husband did not feel a need to visit them frequently. These wives tended to be among the older women in the sample. Only one of the younger husbands did not see his parents at all because of learning of an incestuous relationship in the family.

Couples that saw more of the wife's family tended to do so for one of several reasons. Usually the wife felt closer to her family than to her husband's family, or they lived closer to her family. In instances where both husband and wife each felt closer to their own parents, the wife's preferences tended to trump the husband's preferences. This was due to the fact that the wives were the ones who scheduled holiday gatherings and visits. There were a few instances, though, in which a wife said that *both* she and her husband were closer to her parents than his. In addition, the wife's parents were also more likely to pressure the couple to visit frequently. Consider Vicki's example: "Yes, we go [to my parents' house] for every holiday. There would be trouble if we didn't. . . . It bothers my mother, especially, if I am not there. I would hear about it forever if I did not go. . . . I don't think [my mother] wants her kids to grow up. She wants to know every detail of my life and my brother's life, even about our marriages." Vicki noted that the pressure was on both her and her brother to visit. However, women were more likely to note such pressure in their family, or at least felt more obligated to heed their parents' wishes than men did. While there may have been pressure on the sons to visit their parents, they were more likely to disregard it than the daughters.

MOTHERS' PERCEPTIONS OF VISITS

Mothers were also more likely to say that they saw their daughters and their families more often than their sons and their families. However, the difference in contact was much greater according to the mothers than the adult children.[15] Mothers said that they typically saw their daughters several times a week, while they saw their sons once every few weeks. One mother said, "I see my daughter several times a week. I visit on every Tuesday to see her and the grandchildren and then on weekends we go shopping. . . . I see my sons every few weeks, but I try to talk to him every week. He has his wife now."

A few of the mothers said that they saw their sons more than their daughters. However, these mothers all had highly ambivalent relationships with their daughters. JoAnn, for example, said that she visits her daughter only once a year, and then it is for three days maximum. She described the visits as follows, "You are walking on eggshells the whole time. . . . It is not really conflict . . . it is more guarded. . . . [I] call her the 'Director General.' She is very controlling, judgmental, and volatile. Everyone walks on eggshells around her because of her volatility." In contrast, JoAnn saw her son "every quarter" [year], and he visited her several times a year. Visits were also longer with her son, lasting more like a week. She described her relationship with her son as being excellent because they have very similar personalities.

Although a minority, a significant number of mothers see their sons' families as often as their daughters' families. Interestingly, these tend to be younger mothers with fewer children overall. These mothers spoke frequently about raising their sons to stay close to the family and regularly creating family activities while their children were growing up. They also tended to take the initiative to include their daughters-in-law, as well as their sons-in-law, in the family and to make them feel a part of the family. Diane said, "I see my son as much as my daughter. We meet [where he lives] and go out to dinner with him and his wife. We go kayaking, hiking. . . . We always did things like that as a family when the kids were home. We are all very athletic . . . and outdoorsy. Last weekend we met him at my daughter's house. . . . His wife too."

PHONE CALLS WITH PARENTS AND IN-LAWS

Visits between parents and adult children are often supplemented with phone calls. Not surprisingly, both husbands and wives tend to call their own family more often than their spouse's family. However, women are more likely to call their family than men. Men are also more likely to call their wife's family than women are to call their husband's family. Finally, men are more likely not to talk on the phone at all. As a result, the wife's parents have far more phone contact with the couple than does the husband's parents.

Men were more likely to call their spouse's family when they felt closer to their in-laws than their own parents. This sometimes occurred due to efforts on the part of both their wife and in-laws (see below) or because of an estrangement from their parents.

Marie gave the following example, "[My husband] has always called my parents more or called them first. His family doesn't really have family relations. . . . When I got pregnant, he wanted to call my family first. His family hasn't even called back to congratulate him." These wives tended to have very close families in general, and the husbands were pulled in to the family over time.

Calling in-laws over parents occurred less frequently with women. Many of the women still called their own parents more than their in-laws even when there were problems in their relationship with their parents. Several of the daughters felt that their own mother was judgmental and not as easy to talk to as their mother-in-law, but they still called their mother more often. They said that this was because they felt obligated to call and because they felt more familiar with their own family. As Deb stated, "I used to call my mother every couple of days or drop in to see her with the kids.[16] It was amicable, but we weren't real close. I still called, though. . . . I knew that my parents loved me, but there was no outward affection. . . . We all just went our separate ways. I am very close to my husband's family, though, even though I don't call as much."

Men are less likely to call their parents than women because it is less central to the role of son. In addition, maintaining connections and personal relationships is less important to men's self-identity than women's self-identity.[17] While women are expected to remain close to their parents (i.e., calling and visiting), men are not expected to stay *as* close. In fact, some of the husbands did not talk on the phone to their parents at all. Daughters were less likely to feel like this was acceptable even when there were problems in the relationship. Only one of the wives had no contact with her mother.

These gender differences in calling patterns are consistent with those of previous researchers.[18] Fischer suggests that women may use the phone more than men because of their roles as social manager and kin keeper.[19] That is, they use the phone to keep family members informed of one another and to schedule family gatherings. Women may also use the phone more because of their particular style of social interaction, that is, having more intimate conversations with parents. Therefore, the wife's mother has more knowledge of what the couple is doing and has the potential of being more integrated in their lives than does the husband's mother. Involving husbands in phone conversations with their wife's parents is in fact one mechanism by which they get pulled in to their wife's family.

THE PROCESS BY WHICH MEN GET PULLED IN TO THEIR WIFE'S FAMILY

Men become a part of their wife's family as a result of deliberate efforts of inclusion as well as a day-to-day overlapping of familial circumstances. Consistent with Lee, Spitze, and Logan's hypothesis, men get pulled in to their in-laws' family through their wife.[20] However, men are also drawn in to their in-laws' side of the family through the efforts of their mother-in-law and through their children. Grandchildren tended to have greater contact with their maternal grandparents, which pulled fathers in to the extended family.

Initiatives by the Mothers-in-Law

Many of the mothers-in-law who successfully pulled their sons-in-law in to their family (whether according to the son or to the mother-in-law) said that they started out by including their daughters' boyfriends in family activities from the very beginning. One mother-in-law explained,

> Every time that my daughter brought a new boyfriend home, I said to myself, "He could become your son-in-law . . ." and so I treated each one like a possible son-in-law. . . . They were always invited on all of the family outings, out to dinners, on holidays. . . . We did things that they liked to do too . . . the football game was always on. He and my son went to the gym together. We just treated him like a part of the family from the very beginning.

Mothers said that they did this for both their sons' and daughters' significant others, but their daughters' boyfriends were more likely to "come around" than their sons' girlfriends. The sons' girlfriends were also involved in the family, but just not as much. They assumed that their sons' girlfriends were more involved in their own families. Several of the mothers pointed out that they would not want *their* daughters to spend too much time with their boyfriends' parents because that would "make it look like we are not a close family." Thus, the expectation was that the couple *should* be more involved in the woman's family.

Once the couple was married, the wife's mother continued to include her son-in-law in family events. After marriage, however, the expectation was even greater that the husband would participate in his wife's family. One daughter explained that her family was very upset that her husband did not attend family functions. At first, she tried to hide the fact by saying that he was busy, not feeling well, or had too much work to do. Later it became clear to her family, though, that these were just excuses, and they pressed even harder for him to participate. This put stress on Brenda and Tim's marriage because Tim did not want to spend time with Brenda's family. At the time of the interview, Brenda and Tim were separated. Brenda felt that the expectations of her family had contributed to their separation.

After sons-in-law became a part of the family, the mother-in-law's home tended to become the primary spot to celebrate events, including those for the husband. As a result, he was pulled further in to his wife's family, since her family was included in these events as well. For example, Roseanne explained,

> Just last week my son-in-law got a big promotion. My daughter wanted to have a party for him. . . . My house is bigger than hers and I have more time to do all of the preparation, so we had it here. I suppose his family could have had the party, but my daughter wanted to do it and felt more comfortable asking me. Besides, all of our family lives around here, and his family is east of here.

Initiatives by the Wives

Over and over again, mothers, daughters, and sons said, "A girl [or woman] usually feels more comfortable with her own family." Likewise, most of the men and women said that it was usually the wife who set the couple's social calendar. Wives explained that they would make plans to spend time with their family and usually those plans included their husband as well, although sometimes they did not. Husbands said that they also made plans to see their parents, but it was less likely to include their wife. Instead, they were more likely to stop by for a cup of coffee or to bring the children over to see their parents for short visits. They were less likely, however, to plan family events or extended visits. As a result of wives planning these events, husbands spent more social time overall with their wife's family than their own family.

Many of the couples tried to the divide the holidays "evenly." For example, they might rotate spending each holiday with one versus the other family or they might spend half of the holidays with one family and half with the other family. However, there was a discernible pattern of the couple spending the "heart" of the holiday with the wife's family or the more important holidays with her family. For example, a couple might spend Christmas Eve with his family and Christmas day with her family or Mother's Day morning with his family and Mother's Day afternoon with her family. There was also a tendency for the process to be decided by proximity and driving distance. Here, at least some of the mothers with grandchildren pointed out that being "primary" grandmother (defined as the maternal grandmother) mattered. That is, several of the daughters and sons-in-law moved near her mother after grandchildren were born. As a result, couples spent more of the holidays with her family. Daughters were also more likely to invite their own parents for casual events, such as coming for a weekday dinner. Some of the daughters did say that they invited their in-laws as often as their own parents, but this was not the case for many. As a result, their husband was pulled further in to their family.

Phone calls were another mechanism that pulled men in to their wife's family. Many of the women cited calling one another multiple times throughout the day.[21] As a result, mothers of daughters are more likely to be a part of couples' day-to-day lives than mothers of sons. The mother has a greater connection to what is going on in her daughter's family, including what is going on in her son-in-law's life. While mothers may also be in touch with their sons, they are less likely to draw in their daughters-in-law.

Contact Through the Grandchildren

Several of the (grand)mothers explicitly stated that they considered themselves to be the "primary grandmothers" for their daughter's children, relative to the paternal grandmother. These grandmothers pointed out that they were more likely to be asked by their daughters to assist with child care such as picking grandchildren up after school or going to their daughter's home in the morning to get their grandchildren ready for school if their daughter worked. Mothers felt that their daughters were more likely to ask them for help than they were to ask their in-laws because they were more comfortable with their own mother. Maternal grandparents were also given preference in participating in activities with the daughter and grandchildren (e.g., going to the movies, the beach, or attending the child's school activities). Daughters stated that they were often trying to "kill two birds with one stone" (i.e., spending time with their children and their mother) or that they were more at ease with their mother as compared to their mother-in-law. For example, one daughter-in-law explained,

> I am more likely to invite my mother to the beach with us than my mother-in-law. . . . [She] doesn't like the beach and my mother and I do. Plus, I don't have to be embarrassed if the kids aren't well-behaved or if all I have for their lunch is a peanut butter and jelly sandwich. My mother won't think things or make judgments the way that my mother-in-law might. . . . I can be more relaxed with my mother.

Husbands spend more time with their mother-in-law as a result of the mother-in-law's greater involvement with the children. One son-in-law said,

> My mother-in-law is here every morning after my wife leaves for work. She is usually there making lunches for the kids while I get ready for work . . . so we talk. Usually it is just about what the kids are up to. They are also more likely to go to the kids' games too than my own parents. My own parents aren't big on sports. . . . My wife and I are, though. . . . We are also more likely to just stop by my wife's parents' house than my parents' house or to ask them to go out to dinner at the last minute. . . . We just see more of them. . . . Our lives are more entangled.

One son said that he talked more about his children to his wife's parents than his own parents. One of his children had a disability, and he was more likely to discuss it with his mother-in-law because "she knows him better." Another son said that he feels closer to his wife's parents because of "all that she does for the kids." He stated, "My mother-in-law lives for the girls. Every time that she sees them, she lights up. She buys things for them when we can't. I appreciate that." Another daughter said that her mother stays with her husband and children when she goes away on business trips. She explained, "My husband doesn't mind my mother being there as much as his own mother. My mother lets him take over when he comes home, whereas he sees his mother doing things with the kids that bug him, that remind him of . . . her faults."

ALL IN THE FAMILY

Although couples have greater overall contact with the wife's family than with the husband's family, they do not differentiate in defining who is family. They consider themselves to be as much a part of the husband's extended family as the wife's extended family. Wives were as likely to say that they are members of their husband's family as husbands were to say that they are members of their wife's family. Husbands were also as likely to say that they are still part of their natal family as wives, even though they may not have as much contact. Husbands, though, qualified their definitions of family with statements like, "My parents and sister are still my family, but I have to take care of *this* [emphasis his] family first. The people in this house are *my* family [emphasis his]."

Gender differences in contact, then, do not reflect men's feelings of having left the family or no longer being a part of the family. Nor do they suggest that daughters-in-law do not identify with their husband's family. I will argue, however, that what they do reflect is a cultural assumption that daughters are closer to their parents, which is reflected in spending more time together and the fact that daughters are the ones who arrange the couple's social calendar. I will also argue that the bond of shared motherhood ensures that daughters stay close to their mother.

HOW ARE MEN MORE
CONNECTED TO THEIR WIFE'S FAMILY?

Men get pulled in to their wife's family often while they are still dating or in the first years of marriage. For most of the men, it happens very gradually and is a result of the wife's family's tendency to involve or include them. Only a few of the husbands resisted being pulled in to their wife's side of the family. For example, Vicki and her husband had experienced significant marital problems as a result of his unwillingness to spend more time with her family. Nor were men pulled in to their wife's family if the wife was estranged from her parents. Only one husband had been a significant part of his wife's family but then separated himself from the family as a result of a rift over a shared business venture.

For men, "being pulled in to their wife's family" essentially means seeing them more and socializing with them more than their own family. It also includes spending more holiday time together, sharing more of the children's activities, and sharing more resources. As a result, their lives tended to be more intertwined. For example, Matthew stated, "Well, if I need someone to help me, I am more likely to ask my wife's brother [over my sister's husband]. . . . I see him more. We help each other out . . . like if he needs to borrow my truck. When I built my deck, my wife's father helped me. My father could have, but he lives further away." Although they had been pulled in to their wife's family, the men still stated that they felt closer to their own family. Being pulled in to the wife's family does not mean men lose love or identification with their own family, then. Bill, for example said, "We do more things with my wife's family. They help us more too, but I am still closer to my own mother and sister. I am part of both families, I guess, but I am closer to my own people."

Becoming a part of their wife's family required adjustment on the part of a few husbands. Most commonly, wives said that their husband was resentful when their father first tried to help out around the house or offered advice. One of the wives said, "My husband did not like my father asserting authority on his turf. It was like a test of their masculinity or something, but he has learned to live with it like I have learned to live with his mother's advice about the kids." While most of the husbands seemed to ease in to their wife's family (at least according to them or their wife), others had to make a concerted effort to make a place for themselves in the family. One husband said, "I didn't have anything to do at my mother-in-law's house. I was bored. Then I started fixing up her yard. I liked doing it, and it gave me something to do while I was there." After that point, Ethan said that he started to feel more at home while visiting his in-laws.

SUMMARY AND IMPLICATIONS

Although couples saw more of the wife's parents than the husband's parents, the differences were not large. However, the reasons for seeing more of one set of parents versus the other highlighted the distinctions in intergenerational relationships for men versus women. Couples tended to see either the husband's or the wife's family more when they lived closer. Other than that, the likelihood of seeing the husband's family more than the wife's family increased only when there was a problem with the wife's family and the wife did not want to see her family. Otherwise, the couple saw more of the wife's family. This suggests that greater contact with the wife's family is the default position. In addition, men and women are more likely to report seeing the wife's family more than the husband's family because of pressure from her parents. This implies that parents expect to see more of their daughters, as was verified by the mothers. However, at least some daughters also report that their mothers exert pressure on their brothers too. The fact that none of the men mentioned such pressure indicates either that they may not notice it or that they feel less likely to succumb to it than women. In fact, women called their parents more than their in-laws even when they felt that their mother was harder to talk to than their in-laws. While they may be doing this out of greater familiarity with their own parents, they may also be doing it as part of a greater obligation to keep in touch as daughters versus sons. Another interpretation is that none of the men in the sample actually experienced such pressure from parents, which would suggest that parents have lower expectations of contact with sons than with daughters.

Both men and women telephone their own family more than their in-laws. Consistent with earlier findings,[22] women are more likely to call their family than men, and men are more likely to call their wife's family than women are to call their husband's family. As a result, men are more likely to get drawn in to their wife's family than vice versa. However, these differences occur less often than was anticipated, suggesting that gender roles in the family may be becoming more equal.

Men get pulled in to their wife's family by their mother-in-law, wife, and children. Interestingly, the process begins while adult children are still dating. Mothers conscientiously include potential sons-in-law, as well as potential daughters-in-law, in family activities and holidays. Families expect daughters to stay closer to them than sons, and daughters do so out of familiarity. Husbands then get pulled in to the wife's family, since she is usually the one to arrange get-togethers and holidays and feels an obligation to stay in contact with family even when being with in-laws is more comfortable. The maternal grandmother's greater involvement with grandchildren also further pulls men in to their wife's families. This process varied from months to years, sometimes with greater intensity of involvement over time. Although men were pulled in to the day-to-day lives of their wife's family, most did not, however, feel emotionally closer to their wife's family than their own.

The fact that the differences are not as great as those reported by earlier research implies that gender differences in family roles for adult children may be lessening.[23] Increased expectations of men's involvement in the home and with their own children may transfer to their relationships with their parents as well. Smaller families may also imply that both sons and daughters are expected to stay close to parents. Clearly some vestiges of gender differences remain, but they are not as large as was expected.

The differences that do exist, however, help to explain tensions in mother-in-law and daughter-in-law relationships.[24] There was greater conflict described in instances where the mother-in-law felt that the couple spent significantly more time with the wife's parents. A few of the mothers-in-law also described the jealousy that they felt as a result of having less contact with their son. Whether the poor relationship between mother-in-law and daughter-in-law came before or after the increase in time with the wife's parents was not determined. However, it remains one avenue for daughters-in-law to consider in improving their relationships with in-laws.

The next chapter examines the extent to which mothers feel that they "lose" their sons after marriage. It looks at whether the adage "a daughter is a daughter all of her life, but a son is a son 'til he takes him a wife" is a myth or whether it accurately describes the change in parent and son relationships following marriage. We have seen that couples spend slightly more time with the wife's family, which then pulls the husband in. Do parents of sons then feel that they "lose" their son following marriage, and to what extent does this perception exist? Answering this question will help us to gain a fuller picture of how relationships with adult children change following marriage and how family members perceive those changes.

"A Daughter Is a Daughter All of Her Life, but a Son Is a Son 'til He Takes Him a Wife"

Myth or Reality?

$\mathcal{R}$esults of a recent study of mothers-in-law and daughters-in-law suggest that there is a general assumption in society that while daughters will remain close to their parents following marriage, sons will become independent of their natal family once they are married.[1] Readers commenting on a *Salon* article suggested that this is a highly unfair double standard that disadvantages the parent-son relationship.[2] Sons who stay very close to their mother, in particular, are inappropriately seen as "mama's boys," while such daughters are seen as having healthy ties to their mother. Yet, there is reason to believe that this is more of a stereotype than a social reality. This leads us to ask to what extent this double standard exists in our society, in terms of both expectation and practice within the family. Other evidence of a double standard is the widely acknowledged adage, "A daughter is a daughter all of her life, but a son is a son 'til he takes him a wife." This difference in expectations for sons versus daughters seems surprising in an era in which one would anticipate greater gender equality and less rigid sex roles within the family. The purpose of this chapter is to examine whether or not sons do, in fact, "cut ties" with their natal families following marriage or whether the adage that "a son is a son 'til he takes him a wife" is a myth. The chapter will consider both the existence of this phenomenon occurring in families as well as people's expectations and acceptance of it. The perspectives of both mothers and married children (i.e., sons and daughters) will be examined.

THE MOTHERS' PERSPECTIVE:
IS A SON A SON 'TIL HE TAKES HIM A WIFE?

Moms Who Say "No"

The predominant sentiment among mothers was that it is often the case that a family or mother "loses" her son when he marries but that this had not been the case in their family. Interestingly, many attributed the fact that they remained close to their sons after marriage to their relationships with their daughters-in-law. For example, Maude felt that it was the quality of her relationship with her daughter-in-law that kept her son close to her. She said, "My own brothers do squat [for our parents]. I could not see my son doing that, though. His wife would not let him. She and I have become close too. I have as much of a relationship with my daughter-in-law as my son, well almost as much." Another mother-in-law also said that she did not lose her sons because she had very good daughters-in-law who did not "pull their husbands away." A few of the mothers said that they did not lose their sons, despite the expectation of it happening, because their daughters-in-law wanted to be a part of the family. For example, one of the mothers, Beth, said that her daughter-in-law wanted to be involved in every aspect of their large family because her own family was small and not as close. Because of the eager involvement of her daughter-in-law, Beth felt that she had not lost her son. Thus, daughters-in-law can prevent mothers feeling that they have lost their sons by having a good relationship with their mother-in-law, integrating themselves into the family, or at least not "pulling their husbands away from their families."

Several of these mothers and others also felt that they did not lose their sons because they gave their children "space" to put their own nuclear families first. In addition, they tried not to depend on their children too much, so that their children did not have to choose between them and their own families. Consider Roseanne's example, "I always told my children to put their mate first. I told them, 'Your husband or wife first, and then your parents.' I feel very strongly about that. . . . I don't ask my kids for anything, and maybe that is why [they do not pull away]. I see my friends depend too much on their kids. I don't know what is wrong with people. They need to let their kids live [their own lives]." Phyllis explained her philosophy of giving her children space with the following statement, "You hold your children tight when they are young. When they are grown, you hold them in the palm of your hand. That way, they come back."

Other mothers said that they did not lose their sons despite the fact that it happened to other family members or friends because they raised their sons to stay close to the family. Patty said that her own mother-in-law lost all three of her sons because she did not accept their wives. She explained, "[My mother-in-law] did not want the kids to leave the family, but she ended up shutting them off." As a result, Patty raised her own family to be close-knit. In fact, she still sees each of her five children, who are in their thirties and forties, at least once a day. The children's lives are highly intertwined as well. They spend weekends and at least some weekday evenings together. The in-laws are also friends, and the nieces and nephews transfer from one household to the other with ease. Likewise, Phyllis said that her sons have remained close to the family because they were brought up under the principle of "la familia." She taught them always to help family and to prioritize family, *although to put their spouse and children ahead of even their parents* [emphasis added]. She urged her sons not to be like their uncles who, unmarried, did not attend family events. Phyllis believed that it is the women who must take responsibility for bringing the men in to the family. She said that without the women, men stay focused on "hunting and gathering and doing men things."

Finally, mothers-in-law avoided losing their sons upon marriage by taking initiatives to integrate their daughters-in-law into the family before and/or after the marriage. Patty made a special point to integrate her children's fiancées into the family as soon as the relationship became "serious." She said, "I did not want to lose either of my children, so I included the boyfriend and girlfriend right from the beginning. They were incorporated into the family right from the start. I just felt like the family got bigger. We went from four to eight. . . . The only thing that changed was that they had a ring on their finger." Mary Ann also avoided losing her daughters and sons by being sure to include their spouses in the family. She said that she goes out to lunch sometimes with each of her four children-in-law alone to facilitate their connection to the family. She also hosted a "welcome to the family" party for each of her daughters-in-law when they became engaged to her sons. Many of the daughters-in-law were an integral part of the family. It should be pointed out that this was conscientiously cultivated by the mothers-in-law to prevent their children from pulling away from the family.

Mothers who felt that it was common for a parent to "lose a son" (even though they had not lost theirs) usually pointed to brothers who "went to [their wife's] side of the family." They stated that their own parents "felt like second fiddles" or felt like their families had been replaced. Their parents were missing out on their sons' lives as well as time with their grandchildren. While some accepted this as normative, others were still bitter. What was most interesting, though, was that the women attributed the "loss" as being due to their brothers' movement in to their wives' families rather than a loss of interest in their own natal family.

Thus most of the mothers felt that they had not "lost" their son after marriage, as the adage suggests, despite believing that it often happens in other families. A minority of mothers felt that not only had they not lost their sons after marriage but also the occurrence of this phenomenon in general was a myth. Most, however, believed that you have to work to prevent losing your sons. Pat, for example, felt that she and her husband continued to have close relationships with their sons even after they married, but she felt that this was due to the attitude that she had taken. She explained, "If anything . . . my sons' marriages have enhanced the relationships. It relieves my worry and puts them in a healthy situation. . . . It gives me satisfaction to see that I was a good role model and that they are family oriented and have healthy marriages." Pat did feel that her relationship with her son had changed in one respect, though. She stated, "Your son's main focus isn't you anymore, even if it was before. Your son's main focus should be his wife when he marries. If there is conflict, he should support his wife. If the mother is *smart* [her emphasis], she will accept that. The mother needs a balanced life of her own." She argued that mothers need to take certain steps to ensure that their relationships with their sons continue. She explained, "It behooves us [mothers] to understand what is going on and make the best of it. It is your job to make room for the way that the relationship has changed. Mothers who are too close to the son may feel abandoned. You can never get all of your emotional needs met by your children, though. If the mother has her own life, she can be happy for her son and encourage the relationship." Pat thus recognized the potential of losing her son if she did not anticipate changes in the relationship with him. Lynda also felt that her attitude played an important role in maintaining a good relationship with her son and daughter-in-law. She explained, "I value their independence and respect them as a family which makes *me* more endearing to them."

Mothers believed that they were able to keep their sons close to them through a variety of means. While some conscientiously cultivated a need to be close and a sense of family in their children when they were little, others deliberately gave their children space to have their own families when they were older, and/or they integrated their children's partners into the family. Thus, at least some mothers recognize the potential of losing their sons even when they are young, before they become involved in a serious relationship. They understand that their sons will feel torn if their daughters-in-law do not feel a part of the family or if they do not have the option of putting their own families first when needed. In other words, they recognize the potential for conflict between the nuclear and extended families. Others attributed not losing their sons after marriage to their close relationships with their daughters-in-law or to the fact that they had "good" daughters-in-law. These daughters-in-law did not pull their husband in to their own family exclusively. In contrast, none of the mothers-in-law mentioned their sons explicitly doing anything to prevent a loss of their relationship.

Moms Who Say "Yes"

In contrast to the above, a number of the mothers said that they themselves had experienced "losing" a son when the son married. One of the mothers explained, "Yes, something changes. The son now has to take care of his family. There are expectations of him to do that. It is not that he is no longer your son; he is your son in a different role. With the daughters, the mother/daughter bond is long-standing even though there is a place for the spouse. Daughters do not leave home on the same level."

When mothers were asked whether or not they felt that they had lost their son after his marriage, they were told that this refers to the son "stepping back" from his natal family or "disengaging" from the family. Those mothers who agreed that this had happened were also asked if there were additional ways in which they felt that they had lost their son. Most commonly, mothers stated that their son no longer came by to visit them. This was often the case when there was a problem in their relationship with their daughter-in-law or when the couple spent the majority of their time with the wife's family. These mothers added that when they themselves visited their sons' families, their sons were often working or otherwise away. They felt that they had little or no contact with their sons. Other mothers explained that their sons no longer "belonged" to them after they were married. One mother stated, "They went on their honeymoon, and she kept him!" When I asked her what she meant by that, she said that she no longer had "her son's ear in the evening" or his time after work. She felt that his wife had replaced her. For example, she said that her son no longer needed her to cook for him. Another mother pointed out that you lose your children, both sons and daughters, when they have their own nuclear families of which you are not a part. Overall, however, mothers defined the loss of their son as being due to his commitment to another family, but they felt that this did not happen to as great an extent with daughters.

Many of those who felt that they had "lost" their son believed that it was a natural process in the life course as the adult child becomes the head or cohead of his own family. Janice explained, "I am proud of him that he has the responsibility of home and family [even though they result in him staying away]." However, she said that there is a "little shadow" of her that wishes that he would sometimes stop by for coffee or just to visit. A few of the mothers also confided that they felt some jealousy over their son's greater focus on his wife. Bonnie said that she had to be aware of the jealousy that she felt so that she did not "make things worse" [for her relationship with them] or ruin her son's marriage. She also added, "That is how I raised him, to be a partner with his wife and to think of her first. It is the right thing, but I don't have to like it. I would kill him if it were anything less, [though]."

At least some of these mothers also believed that there were advantages to this norm of sons leaving the family upon marriage. Despite the fact that Camilla wished that her son would stop by more, she stated, "I am thankful that it is the way to live, though; I was a wife once too. My husband's support for me was always unbelievable. . . . I was fortunate to have *all* of him. He visited his family, but he wasn't there at their beck and call." Thus, according to Camilla, the advantage of this arrangement is to the *couple* and to the wife in particular, rather than to the mother-son relationship.

Mothers also pointed out that you do not totally lose your son, however. Camilla felt that the love between her and her son was still there even though his focus was elsewhere. For Camilla, then, the "loss" was a matter of degree. Her son's priority was no longer her, and his time with her was significantly diminished as well. Likewise, his relationship with her now included his wife and children.

Is "A Daughter a Daughter All of Her Life?"

The first part of the statement, that "a daughter is a daughter all of her life," rang true to all of the mothers. They felt that daughters remain closer to their parents and are more integrated into the household than sons. They explained that their daughters were more emotionally attached to the family than their sons and called more often than sons when they left home. Others added that daughters stayed closer to them because they shared pregnancy and mother-hood. Although Sally felt that she lost her son when he became the head of his own family, she did not believe that her daughter's acquisition of a family had the same effect. She explained, "Daughters also become cohead [of their own family], but you don't lose your daughter so much because motherhood provides you a connection to other mothers." While not all of the mothers believed that their daughters were closer to them (and their husband) than their sons, the majority did and felt that it was an integral characteristic of the daughter's role.

As was explained in chapter 4, many of the mothers believed that couples tend to go with the wife's family more frequently than to the husband's family. They explained that this was because wives prefer to be with their own families out of familiarity and that husbands are willing to accommodate this. Barbara explained, "It is because he [the son] wants to get along with and please his wife. Girls don't want to be with their husband's family; they want to be with their own family." Women also recognize that this practice of spending more time with the wife's family is socially acceptable. They can spend more time with their own family without breaking the expectations of the daughter-in-law role. The mothers believed that "women usually rule the roost" on these matters and are the ones to set the couple's social calendar. As a result, couples spend more time with the wife's family.

THE SONS' PERSPECTIVE

In contrast to what the mothers said, most of the married men agreed that the adage "a son is a son 'til he takes him a wife" accurately described the change in their relationship with parents when they married. A minority, however, felt that they had not stepped back from their natal family or "cut ties" with it. In fact, Ed pointed out that he was much closer to his mother since he married than he ever had been before. He ran away from home several times in high school and lived away from home while he was a young adult, but he settled in the area when he married. He is the one who cares for his mother now. In contrast, his wife had significantly curtailed her relationship with her parents because of an ongoing feud between her husband and parents. Only one of the sons equivocated on his answer. He felt that he was not as close to his parents as his sister was, but that they were still his family. He explained, "Work and [my nuclear] family come first, but they are still my family too."

The majority of sons, however, believed that the adage accurately described the change in their relationship with their parent(s) after marriage. Samuel, who is poor and unemployed, explained, "I think it is true. The wife takes over as the mother figure. She does things for the husband that the mother would do. My mother and I were very close, but if she were alive I would be closer to my wife still. It would be a prerequisite that my mother would have to love my wife too."

Stephen, who is a professional, also pointed to the need to concentrate on his own family over his parents and siblings, who live in the area. He stated, "I am still a son and brother, but it is after being a husband and father. I have my own family, which has to come first. My parents and brothers and sisters need me too, but it can't be as much. . . . Daughters stay closer to their parents. Sons stay close too, but they have responsibilities to their own families. You want them to be a little more independent."

Mike, another professional, felt that he also detached somewhat from his family of origin to focus on taking care of his own nuclear family. Mike was motivated by his religious ideals. He explained, "The Bible says that man is to cleave to his wife, not his mother, and be responsible for his own family. I try to live a moral life, and that means taking care of my family first." Colin, too, felt that he had to concentrate on "his own house and his own family and his goal of joining the fire department" once he married. For all of these sons, focusing on their own family meant "detaching" at some level from their natal family.

There were some class and educational differences. Middle- and upper-middle-class sons who were more highly educated tended to distance themselves more from their natal family. In contrast, sons from working-class families tended to maintain closer ties with their parents following marriage. This is likely due to the emphasis placed on the extended family for working-class children while they are growing up.[3] It may also be due to the greater need to share resources in the working-class family and the exposure to new ideas among the educated middle and upper-middle classes.

THE DAUGHTERS' PERSPECTIVE

What about the married women? To what extent did they think that the adage fit their own husband's experience? The women were more likely than the men to say that the adage did *not* describe their experience. They said that their husband (and/or brothers) have remained close to their parents and have not disengaged from the family. For example, Kathy, who is now divorced, said, "It is the opposite in my family. My brothers are on my mother like glue. They both will go and help her do something at the drop of a hat. My mother stays at my older brother's camp a lot too. They do everything for her. . . . My husband stayed very close to his parents too. They still share a triple-decker."

In contrast, a substantial number of the women felt that their husband did pull away from his natal family when they married and that it is typical. One of the women said, "I think that it [the adage] is true. My husband and brothers were not close to their mothers. My own daughters are closer than my sons. . . . My boys have their own lives. . . . My husband did not have ties [to his family]. We went to his mother's house when we were invited, though . . . about once a month."

Other women said that the men in their family tended to "go with their wives" and that they were not *as* close to their parents as the women in their family. It wasn't until her own son married, though, that Amy felt the full impact of the adage. She stated,

> I believe it [the adage] now. I have stayed close to my daughter since she married, but not my son. They [the son, daughter-in-law, and grandson] never come. I tell my son that we want to see them, and he says, "I have to check with [daughter-in-law's name]." But they never come. I have to talk

to him at work now [rather than calling his home]. Sometimes he comes without his wife. . . . He is a different person when she is around. He is torn, the poor kid. . . . They have always spent more time with her family. I don't complain about it. I just say that I want to see them when I have not seen them for awhile.

As for her own husband, she explained, "Well, I suppose that the adage applies to him too, but it had more to do with their family not being close rather than me being unwilling to visit. It was like he got married and they just said good-bye. . . . They did not call on birthdays because they assumed that I would do it. . . . That kind of thing." Finally, a minority of the women said that their husband was detached from their family but that they were like that even before they married.

SUMMARY AND IMPLICATIONS

A majority of the overall respondents felt that the adage "a son is a son 'til he takes him a wife" did not describe the changes in their relationship (or their husband's relationship) as mothers, sons, and wives following marriage. Some of these family members said that they thought the adage was true in general, but that it did not describe their situation. Sons, however, were most likely to say that they had pulled away from their natal family because either they needed to focus on their own family when they married or because their life was now with their spouse. Fewer of the mothers and wives felt that it described their situation with their sons (or their husband's situations with his mother). Nearly all of the mothers stated that they remained close to their daughter after marriage because daughters tend to stay more connected to the family and because they eventually share motherhood.

Whether they felt that they had "lost" their son when he married (that is, the son had pulled away, disengaged, or stepped back from his natal family) or not, mothers as well as adult children noted a change in the relationship between parents and sons following marriage. Mothers who did not feel that they had lost their son believed that it was often because they had a good relationship with their daughter-in-law or that their daughter-in-law wished to be a part of the family. To an extent, then, it was up to the daughters-in-law. Some of the mothers-in-law also pointed out that it was in their best interest to make way for the daughter-in-law in the relationship and to make a point of including her in the family as early as possible, and so they did. Thus, the relationship with the son changed by the inclusion of the daughter-in-law. Sons felt less involved in their natal family and more involved in their own family (i.e., their wife and children) and their wife's natal family. The extent to which sons pulled away from their natal family was a matter of degree and dependent on both the prior relationship and the daughter-in-law's relationship with his family.

It is interesting to note that sons are more likely to believe that they have pulled away from their natal family than daughters or mothers. This may be the result of the social expectation or the prevalence of the myth of "cutting ties" for sons. That is, sons internalize the belief that they should pull away from their natal family as part of becoming independent adults in order to concentrate on their own nuclear family when they marry.

Many of the respondents pointed to the inevitability of sons *lessening* ties with their natal family. Mothers pointed out that it was a "natural process" and something to be expected. They stated that they had raised their sons to put their own families first. While daughters were also raised the same way, it was expected that they could and would stay more involved in the natal family while doing so. The fact that women shared motherhood and that daughters maintained closer ties after leaving the home (i.e., visiting and calling) accounted for much of this. These results suggest the continued importance of the nuclear family. Despite our assumption that nuclear families are "not so nuclear,"[4] we continue to expect and promote them. This includes the expectation that sons and daughters will prioritize their nuclear family over their natal family.

But why is the nuclear family so important in our society? I argue that the nuclear family and its presumed independence from the extended family is a result of several things, including our society's emphasis on individuality and self-reliance. The family unit has always been a source for socializing children according to the society's values. The ideals of a nuclear family, then, are important for a country that promotes personal responsibility. The nuclear family is also the result of the transition from marriage being based on an alliance between extended families to love-based companionate and individualistic marriages.[5] No longer does the extended family have a vested interest in a child's marriage. The focus in marriage is on one's relationship to spouse and children to a much greater degree than it was in the past. Thus, the nuclear family, and not the extended family, is the primary focus for adult children.

Why, then, are daughters not also expected to pull away from the family to the same degree that sons are? Mothers and daughters overwhelmingly pointed to their shared motherhood as a bond that kept them close. Sons, however, did not talk about a shared bond of fatherhood with their father. The bond of motherhood and the acceptance of couples spending more time with the wife's family than the husband's family all resulted in this greater tie to the wife's family and the pulling away, to various degrees, of the son from his natal family. This will be discussed in greater detail in the next chapter.

The extent to which sons did pull away, though, did not support the expectation of a universal "loss" of one's son upon marriage. Many respondents reported continued close mother-son ties following marriage. A number of mothers said that their own husband and brothers had pulled away from their natal family, but their sons had not. This suggests that the gender difference in mothers' relationships with sons versus daughters may be lessening and that sons' and daughters' roles in the nuclear family are becoming more gender neutral. As a result, changes in men's and women's relationships with their parents are not as different as expected.

Interestingly, the majority of the sons did feel that they had stepped back from their natal family in order to focus on their own family. It is unlikely that this means men's feelings of responsibility to their spouse and children are greater than women's. Instead, it may reflect a feeling of not being *as close* to their natal family as their wife is to hers or an internalization of the myth of separation. Additionally, women may be able to fulfill their obligations of wife and mother while still being connected to their natal family while for men, there is greater exclusivity in the two roles.

In what ways is the daughter-and-wife/mother role less exclusive than the son-and-father/husband role? It is the wife and mother's main responsibility to serve as the connecting link to parents and grandparents for her children and husband.[6] That would include the work involved in maintaining links to her own parents, as well as to her husband's parents. In addition, although the majority of mothers of young children work outside of the home, provision for the nuclear family is a more central aspect of masculinity than it is of femininity for a married couple.[7] Provision for the nuclear family is in many ways at odds with maintaining close ties with one's parents. It requires significant investment in one's career or job and focus on maintaining a home. While mothers, too, maintain career and home, they are the ones who also maintain ties and relationships and for whom provision is not as central to gender identity.[8] This will be discussed in greater detail in the next chapter.

In short, do mothers "lose" their sons when they marry? Losing a son after marriage does occur in a substantial number of families, but it is not universal. Nor do the majority of men and women believe that this should be the case or think that it would be fair. Mothers who feel that they have "lost" their sons see them as no longer "belonging" to them because of their movement and commitment to another family. This includes a significantly greater focus on their own nuclear family and relatively more involvement in their wife's natal family.[9] The next chapter will discuss the way in which marriage changes parent and adult child relationships, even for mothers who feel that they have not lost their son, and explores the causes of these changes overall.

What do these results, then, tell us about the greediness of marriage? For many men, marriage (and even more so, parenthood) requires their full attention. As one son said, "Sons stay close too, but they have responsibilities to their own families. You want them to be a little more independent." Many of the mothers said that once their sons were married, their attention and focus were now on their wives rather than their parents and siblings. In fact, mothers even thought that this is the way that it should be, that marriage or perhaps their wives should consume their attention. This suggests the importance that we place on marriage, even if it is greedy. It further suggests that we value individualistic marriages. That is, we expect people to focus on their partner and to fulfill their partner's needs.

Marriage, however, does not appear to be as greedy an institution for women, at least as it regards their parents. Mothers were less worried about interrupting their daughters' time with their husbands in the evening than they were worried about interrupting their sons' time with their wives. Marriage may not disrupt the parent–adult child relationship as much for daughters because the wife's role includes being the conduit to the extended family, including her parents. While wives devote a great deal of themselves to their husband and children, they do so within the context of their extended family. The increased contact that couples have with the wife's parents versus the husband's parents means that marriage is less greedy for parent–adult child relationships. The impact of this difference in intergenerational relationships over the life course will be discussed in the concluding chapter.

· 6 ·

The Effect of Marriage on Intergenerational Relationships

*N*ot surprisingly, major life course transitions for both parents and children have a significant effect on parent–adult child relationships. Among parents' life course transitions, both parental divorce and declines in parental health lead to deteriorating relationships.[1] The effects of adult children's life course transitions, however, begin as early as the age at which children leave home. In particular, parents report a lessening of conflict and power issues but do not feel as close to their children when they leave home.[2] Relationships with both parents improve for women when they get married but worsen as a result of divorce or problems in the daughter's marriage. The effect of a son's marriage is not so straightforward, however. In fact, it is never-married sons who have better relationships with both parents in comparison to married, divorced, or separated sons. Sons' marital problems and divorce lead to a deterioration in relationships with fathers, but not with mothers.[3] Thus gender plays a central mediating role in the effect of adult children's marriage. A child's marriage worsens a mother's relationship with a son, while it improves her relationship with a daughter. What is it about the marriage of a son and/ or the mother-son relationship that causes this difference?

HOW MARRIAGE AFFECTS
RELATIONSHIPS WITH SONS VERSUS DAUGHTERS

Earlier research suggests that a daughter's relationship with both of her parents improves following marriage while a son's relationship with his mother worsens following marriage.[4] However, half of the mothers in this study reported that relationships with neither sons nor daughters changed following their children's marriage—although one mother reported that her *daughter's* relationship with her son changed after he married because the daughter could not get along with her sister-in-law. These mothers did note other status transitions that changed the relationship, though, such as the child moving out of the house or having his or her own children (and therefore having less time). Several of the mothers said that their children's medical problems, which included depression, also affected their relationships. Another mother said that her relationship with her son was greatly changed when she witnessed the results of his assault on his wife. She said, "He might be my son, but I could not condone that . . . and he knew it. He pulled away and distanced himself. . . . and I did not see him for months. He knew he had disgraced himself and the family."

In contrast, nearly half of the mothers said that their relationships with their sons worsened after marriage. Most of these women said that the relationship with their son but not their daughter had worsened. One of the moms explained, "My relationship with my son isn't as close now. I want to call, but I have to think about his family time. I have to be sensitive to his wife and the fact that she wants to be with him." This mother did not make a parallel comment about her son-in-law's need for time with her daughter, however. Another mother stated,

> You have heard the saying, "A son is a son 'til he takes him a wife?" That would describe how it changed. I don't disagree with it. He did a lot which took time away from [my husband] and I. . . . It wasn't just about having enough time, [though]. It was an emotional pulling away too. . . . We feel strongly that you bring your children up to be independent and have their own lives. . . . They should have their own holidays and family customs and their own core family. . . . With daughters you stay more connected because you share motherhood.

The other mothers said that their relationships with both their sons and daughters were not as close following marriage. Dawn said that she was not as close to her daughter, Kathy, because Kathy's husband was now her daughter's best friend. She explained, "I admire the way that she has made a family based on *their marriage*, though." As for her son, Steve, she said, "They went on a honeymoon, and she [the daughter-in-law] kept him! I have to needle my way in once a week. . . . She is a great cook, so he doesn't even need me to feed him. He is not *my* [her emphasis] baby anymore, but I know it is supposed to be like that." Lynda also said that her daughter became more private following marriage, and her son had to "figure out how to [still] have a relationship" with her. She explained, "It [the relationship] evolved. . . . He had to figure out who was going to come first now, me or his wife . . . how to balance having a mother and a wife. He wasn't sure of how to be close to me anymore. Plus, he had a mother-in-law too now, and he wasn't sure of how to deal with the holidays. Everything was new. He was becoming angry and frustrated."

Surprisingly, a minority of the mothers said that their relationships with their sons improved following their marriages. These moms said that their relationships with their sons were better because they were more involved with the (extended) family since they married. They were not out with their friends as much. Several of the mothers also said that their daughters-in-law were responsible for their being closer to their sons because they were "such good daughters-in-law." They explained that their daughters-in-law made an effort to facilitate their relationships with their sons and to include them in family events.

Younger mothers and those with fewer children were more likely to say that their sons' marriages had not changed their relationships with them. One of the younger mothers said, "We had only two children, one son and one daughter. So I made sure that I was close to both of them." These mothers also talked more about their relationships with their sons when they were teenagers and were more reflective about their sons in general. They tended to spend more family time together and to raise their sons and daughters similarly with respect to family values. For example, when asked to compare her relationship with her son versus her daughter, Patty said,

> I am very close to both. It is the same feeling. I tell my daughter that she is my favorite daughter, and I tell my son that he is my favorite son. . . . I have never had to [depend on them], but they both would [be emotionally supportive]. My son may be a little more sensitive and helpful that way. . . . [His marriage] made us even closer. Now he was grown up, not a bachelor anymore. His wife bonded us even closer.

While this suggests a significant shift in the nature of mother-son ties across time, it is important to remember that these ties are still embedded within an overall cultural expectation of gender differences in intergenerational relationships. Thus, we still see some gender differences in intergenerational relationships for younger mothers. For example, one mother said, "My son and I have an excellent relationship . . . now. It was not always like that though. Things were horrible for about five years in his teens. . . . [She describes those years at length.] [But] I would say that I am less connected to my son, only because I know less about him emotionally." This was true even though Sophie talked to her son at length and spent a significant amount of time with him as an adult.

Sons who were the only child in the family for some period of time had relationships with mothers that tended to be very close. Jean explained, "My relationship with him is probably the most important because he was the first child and a boy. I was a single mom and lived in the apartment above my parents. It is a very close bond because it was really just the two of us for the first couple of years." Despite being very close to her oldest son, though, Jean felt that marriage had still changed their relationship. She said, "He keeps apologizing because he feels that his wife, Valerie, has replaced me. He always says, 'Valerie and I' or 'we.' I tell him that I understand, that he is a man now and has his own life."

The most important factor that affected whether and how marriage changed a mother's relationship with her son was the nature of the mother-in-law and daughter-in-law relationship at marriage. Stacey was very distraught that she did not see more of her son and his family. She stated that she had not seen much of her son since he married. Stacey said, "[My daughter-in-law] was always on the cooler side. . . . Everything has always been her family. . . . She could be jealous. She comes, but you can tell that she doesn't want to." Strained relationships between mother-in-law and daughter-in-law make it difficult for a son to maintain intergenerational relationships similar to what they were before marriage if his wife does not want to spend time with his mother. Other studies of mother-in-law and daughter-in-law relationships have also found that conflict in the relationship and negative feelings on the part of either party make sons/husbands feel torn.[5] Not surprisingly, as a result, these men often spend less time with their mother rather than their wife. In a few situations, conflict between in-laws led to separation, divorce, or the possibility of divorce. For example, Colin was not sure if his marriage would continue if his wife were not more willing to allow his parents to visit.

WHAT IS IT ABOUT A RELATIONSHIP WITH A SON THAT CHANGES WHEN HE MARRIES?

Chapter 5 described how some mothers felt that they had lost their son after he married. They believed that their son no longer "belonged" to them like he once had and that their son had his own nuclear family, of which they were not a part. These sons did not come by to visit, and they were often gone when their mother visited them and their family. In contrast, the majority of the mothers felt that they had not lost their son but that the relationship had changed to some degree. This section will describe the nature of that change.

Overwhelmingly, mothers pointed out that their sons' priority and focus were now elsewhere. For example, one mother said,

He used to be more focused on our family: us, his aunts and uncles, and his cousins. On holidays, his priority was to be with us. He likes to do outdoor work, and he would do projects around our yard. His focus now is more on his wife and kids and his job. They are his priority . . . and his own house. If there is something for our family but his wife has other plans, we don't see him.

This was similar to many of the mothers' comments that their sons did not come by to visit as often. Mary, for example, said, "My son was always here for every family get-together and vacation, no matter where he lived or what he was doing. Since he was married, though, he doesn't make nearly the effort. He lives near his wife's family, and they stay there for holidays. Plus, he can never get off work now because his vacation days are spent going away with them." Mothers who felt that they had lost their sons said that their sons did not come by to visit at all. The difference, then, was a matter of the degree of change. Mothers did say, however, that having their son's priority and focus be elsewhere was the biggest change and the hardest one for them to get used to. One mother referred to this change as follows: "[My husband and I] are no longer my son's world . . . to the extent that we were. His wife, and his home, and his job are his world now, and that is okay with me."

Mothers also said that their sons no longer consulted them (or their husbands) about matters like they had before they were married. While this could also be the result of the son's maturation, mothers pointed out that their sons' decisions were now made in conjunction with their wives. Mary said,

I used to be my son's best friend . . . I think. We would talk everything over. Now I hear about things only after the fact. I am glad that he has his wife to talk to . . . and she has a level head. But hearing about things after the fact, I feel like I am not as big a part of his life. Plus, I worry about some of the changes he has made. . . . I worry that he has [made] mistakes.

A few of the mothers felt shut out of their sons' lives, although many did not. Those who did not were usually the ones who were more proactive about including their daughters-in-law (and sons-in-law) in the family. Those parents that felt that they were still a part of their sons' lives usually included their daughters-in-law as well.

Interestingly, one of the mothers said that parents *should* no longer be privy to their children's business once they are married. Carol pointed out that the mother-in-law is not "in the marriage." She explained, "The mother-in-law has to make up her mind that she is not in the marriage. The minister said, 'You are now man and wife, not man and wife and mother-in-law.' I believe that [my kids'] marriages are not my business. . . . What is going on in their lives is between them and their spouses, and I don't want to know about it."

Only a few of the mothers talked about the effect of the child's marriage on the overall family or the married child's relationships with siblings. Most of the mothers instead focused on their own relationships with their children. Those who did talk about the implications for the family as an entity usually focused on the measures that they took to keep the family close. Only a few of the mothers said that their son's relationship with his siblings had changed.

Finally, mothers pointed out that their son's marriage changed their relationship because it now included his wife as well. For some mothers, this was a very positive addition, while others saw it as an infringement on their ties with their son. Mary complained, "I don't have any access to my son alone! They share the same e-mail account, and I am supposed to call them both at home rather than calling on his cell phone. I feel like I don't have *my* [her emphasis] boy anymore!" In sharp contrast, one of the mothers stated, "It has been a gift, having Kathy come into our lives. She has been very good for our son, and she has improved our relationship with him because he is focused more on family time. I feel like I have two daughters now, not just one." The addition of a third person, then, has the potential to strengthen the relationship by embracing the changes in the son's life, but it also has the potential of weakening it by coming between the mother and son. Thus, the effect is highly dependent on the mother-in-law's perspective and her stance toward her daughter-in-law and her son's marriage.

Mothers were often at a loss for words when asked to explain further what the inclusion of a daughter-in-law in their relationship with their son actually meant for them. Some said that it meant that she was often around when their son was around and that she was a part of family gatherings and of the family in general. Others said that their love for their son now had to extend to their daughter-in-law. Most of the mothers-in-law said that they loved their daughters-in-law and that this was not a hardship. Those that did not get along with their daughter-in-law found that extending affection was difficult and required effort on their part. In some instances they were not able to include her, and this caused conflict. A few mothers were also able to articulate that the inclusion of their daughter-in-law in their relationship with their son meant that the son was no longer "hers alone" and that the nature of the relationship was no longer "one-on-one exclusively."

Mothers noted fewer changes in their relationships with their daughters following marriage. The biggest change that they noticed was that the daughter no longer had as much time to visit. A few mentioned that they were no longer their daughter's main confidant, but they did not suggest that their daughter's focus and priority were elsewhere. This may be the result of the continued closeness between parents and daughters across the life course.[6] For women, relationships with parents are paramount and close to the top of the hierarchy of obligations, while men do not give the same kind of priority to their own parents.[7] Mothers also did not say anything about their relationships with their daughters now including their sons-in-law. The presence of the sons-in-law did not change the nature of the exclusive mother-daughter bond.

MOTHER-RELATIONSHIPS

What is it about the mother-son relationship that causes it to change following marriage? That is, why does marriage make mother-son relationships worse? The vast majority of the mothers did not say that they were any closer to their sons than their daughters while they were growing up. However, the mother-son relationship changes to a greater degree following marriage than does the mother-daughter relationship. As was shown in chapter 4, there is some tendency to have more contact with the wife's family following marriage than the husband's family and for the husband to be "pulled in" to the wife's family. In addition, the son's marriage means greater inclusion of the in-laws than does the daughter's marriage. It changes the nature of the relationship to a greater degree. Mothers and daughters remain close due to shared motherhood and the societal expectation to be close, both of which are absent in the mother-son relationship. Instead, the daughter-in-law *joins* the mother-son relationship, eliminating its exclusivity and changing the nature of the relationship. I argue that much of this is due to the centrality of relationships in women's identities.[8] Daughters-in-law are more likely to be part of the relationship because relationships are more important to them, both their relationship to their husband and to their in-laws. In fact, many daughters-in-law are disappointed when their relationship with their mother-in-law is not better.[9] Mothers-in-law also expect this closer relationship, hence the reason why Mary Ann threw "welcome to the family" parties for her daughters-in-law but not for her sons-in-law.

WHY DO DAUGHTERS STAY CLOSER?

Mothers overwhelmingly agreed with the statement "a daughter is a daughter all of her life." The vast majority described very deep and loving relationships. Their faces would light up when they discussed their daughters. Some lamented that they did not see their daughters as often as they would like (particularly if they lived far away). Only a few believed that their relationship with their daughter was not as strong as it was before they married. These mothers felt that their daughters' husbands were now their best friends, and as a result, the relationship was not quite as close as it had been. Despite this, Dawn exclaimed, "I admire the way that she has made a family based on their marriage, though."

Not all of the mothers were as close to their daughters as they would like to be, however. A few mothers described problematic relationships that they felt were due to their daughters' distant or volatile personalities. One of the mothers felt that her daughter's remoteness was due to the fact that she had to work so much while her daughter was growing up, and as a result, the daughter had to assume responsibility for her younger brother. These mothers felt that the relationship had always been distant, however, and had not changed following their marriages.

All of the daughters who were interviewed discussed the need to stay close to their parents. Even Ruth, whose mother was an alcoholic and had neglected and mentally abused her daughter, tried to maintain a close relationship with her mother by calling daily and often talking for hours at a time. A few of the daughters stated that their family was not close, but that they visited and called anyway. Kathy was embarrassed to see or call her mother because she was recently divorced, but she felt obligated to do so nevertheless.

Daughters stay closer to parents because it is a central component of the daughter role. Girls are socialized to cultivate and value emotional ties with family members, and this pattern remains as they become young adults.[10] While sons are encouraged to be more independent at an early age, parents of daughters are more likely to emphasize relational connectedness.[11] Although both men and women report higher affective closeness to their own parents than to in-laws, the difference is greater for women than for men.[12] In fact, women express stronger filial norms than men from young adulthood to old age[13] and provide more emotional support to both parents and in-laws.[14] Thus, women are also more involved in kin networks and parent-child relationships because they place greater emphasis on close emotional bonds with family and because they perform the gendered work of kin keeping.[15] As a result of daughters remaining closer to parents, however, they pull their husbands in to their own kin networks leaving the mothers of sons sometimes feeling like they have "lost" a son. The relative difference in what one can expect of a daughter versus a son also exaggerates one's perception of the actual difference in behavior.

SUMMARY AND IMPLICATIONS

Results of this research suggest that nearly half of mothers believe that their relationships with both their sons and daughters did not change as a result of their marriages. A small majority even says that their relationship with their sons improved following marriage, due in part to their daughters-in-law and in part to their sons becoming more family oriented following marriage. Nearly half, though, say that the relationship with their son worsened, while most of these say that their relationship with their daughter did not.

Why then does marriage worsen a mother's relationship with her son but not her daughter? Relationships with sons appear to change to a greater degree when a son marries versus when a daughter marries. As was proposed in the last chapter, a child's priority and focus are shifted more for sons than for daughters. In addition, the relationship between the mother and son seems to include his spouse more so than the relationship between the mother and daughter. While daughters, too, need to focus on their own nuclear family, they are able to maintain relationships with parents to a greater degree than sons. This is the result of the greater emphasis that women place on intergenerational ties and their kin-keeping activities. It is also the result of the fact that couples spend more time with her family following marriage than his family as was discussed in chapter 4. In fact, mothers were more likely than adult children to state that their sons spent more time with their wife's family than with their own family. Finally, the difference may in part be due to the greater exclusivity in the roles of son and husband versus daughter and wife.

Men's experience as husband and father in American society still require him to focus significantly on the role of provider.[16] It is provision for the nuclear family rather than the extended family, however, that defines men's identity. Even when parents require care, sons' contributions are often limited to circumscribed assistance rather than daily personal care activities that are performed by daughters.[17] Work and the provision of home, are often in contrast with concentrating on one's extended family. While women, too, are more focused on work than ever, their roles as mother and wife are more consistent with maintaining close relationships with extended family. That is, women's roles as wife and mother include being the conduit for their husband's and children's relationships with extended family. The kin work of wife and mother make the roles of wife and daughter less exclusive than the roles of husband and son.

Mother-son relationships are changing, however. Younger mothers and those with fewer children were less likely to say that their relationship with their son had worsened after he married. This was due in part to their attempts to include their daughters-in-law in the family and a greater focus on the entire family spending time together. However, the change is also likely due to a lessening of the gendered nature of parent-child relationships. That is, parents treat sons versus daughters more similarly than ever before and expect more similar relationships than they have in the past. Parents are less likely to believe that sons will cut off ties with family following marriage. They are more likely to cultivate their relationships with their sons while they are growing up and expect them to remain close. Likewise, men are more involved in family life than ever before.

The status transition to marriage does in fact affect many intergenerational relationships, but not all. It has a greater impact on mother-son relationships than mother-daughter relationships. Why, though, are status transitions so important to the parent-child bond? Status transitions usually require a change in the nature of the relationship or a realigning of relationships within the overall family. While change can be positive, it often leads to conflict or ambivalence in the relationship as family members learn to adjust. As children become more independent, parents become more dependent, and as other family members enter the picture, parents and adult children need to change their way of relating to one another and their expectations of one another. While some families are able to adapt to such change relatively quickly, others cannot, and the conflict is drawn out.

Daughters-in-law had an important mediating effect on whether or not mother-son relationships changed after marriage. Some of the mothers felt that their relationships with their sons did not change because they had "good" daughters-in-law. What they meant by this was that the daughter-in-law's presence did little to change the nature of the relationship. For example, these daughters-in-law did not pull their husbands in to their side of the family or arrange for the couple to spend more time with her family than his family. Other mothers-in-law went out of their way to include their daughters-in-law in the family, again minimizing the disruption of their relationships with their sons. All of this suggests that what is most disruptive in the status transition called marriage is the new role that the daughter-in-law will play. This matters because of the importance of relational connectivity to women.[18]

The changes following marriage leave many challenges for mothers, fathers, and other family members who wish to maintain intergenerational ties. The next chapter will focus on these challenges and the initiatives that mothers take to maintain bonds with adult married children.

· 7 ·

The Challenge for Mothers in Parent–Adult Child Relationships

*M*others play a central and unique role in intergenerational families. Both sons and daughters report more positive relationships with their mother than with their father,[1] although the differences are greater for daughters.[2] Mothers also report having more positive but not more negative relations with their children than fathers.[3] In fact, the mother and daughter relationship is the closest of all intergenerational relationships.[4]

Women are also more involved than men in maintaining intergenerational relationships across adulthood, both as mothers and as daughters.[5] Women express stronger obligations, are more likely to maintain family ties, and are more involved in assistance and caregiving.[6] Women, thus, serve as the family "kin keeper." They take responsibility both for setting the family's social calendar as well as doing the "kin work" to facilitate close relationships. The former includes negotiating visits with extended family over the holidays, inviting them for additional visits and meals throughout the year, and including them in the children's activities. The latter "kin work" encompasses the activities that go into maintaining relationships, which often may feel like work. This includes keeping in touch through phone calls and visits, overseeing that the grandchildren maintain contact, keeping grandparents updated on the grandchildren's activities, and attempting to create an atmosphere that minimizes conflict. Earlier researchers have argued that because women perform the kin work and are more involved in the kin network, that they may control men's (and arguably, children's) access to family.[7] Others suggest that mothers are more involved in adult child–parent relationships because they place greater importance on close emotional bonds with family members.[8]

Despite, or perhaps because of, women's closer relationships with their children, they are often the brunt of in-law jokes.[9] The stereotype of the

71

mother-in-law is one of an overbearing, overly protective, and sometimes controlling interloper in the couple's marriage. Popular psychology emphasizes the need for the mother to "let go" of her children in adulthood and the difficulty that can come with this. The evidence for this is the abundance of self-help books on the topic.[10] The mother is more often than the father thought of as pining away for her grown children who have left the nest.

Being the closer parent can negatively affect relationships with adult children. Adult children, particularly daughters, report greater ambivalence, or feelings of both positive and negative sentiments, with mothers than with fathers.[11] Life course transitions also impact the relationship. For example, a daughter's relationship with her mother improves after marriage, perhaps as a result of shared roles, but worsens following divorce. In contrast, a son's relationship with his mother worsens following marriage and improves following divorce.[12]

The purpose of this chapter is to examine the role of the mother in her changing relationship with her son. Chapter 4 showed the significant part that mothers play in incorporating their sons-in-law into the family and their ability to maintain close relationships with their sons by giving them space and making their daughters-in-law feel welcome after marriage. As was discussed in chapter 6, however, the relationships with their sons change significantly for many mothers, sometimes worsening after marriage. How do these mothers handle the changes in their relationships with their sons? How do they manage the loss or the lessening of their ties with their sons when they occur? The results discussed in this chapter are based on the mother's perspective only.

NEGOTIATING THE CHANGES
IN RELATIONSHIPS WITH SONS

The methods for maintaining close relationships with adult children following marriage were discussed in chapter 4. But how do mothers respond when they are not as close as they would like to be with their sons, when they feel that they have at least partially "lost" their sons? Interestingly, many of the women felt contradictions within their own set of values. For example, Bonnie felt at odds about the kind of husband that her son, Davey, was. She explained, "I am proud of him that he has the responsibility of home and family . . . even though it means he isn't here." However, she also admitted that she felt jealousy toward her daughter-in-law, Ashley, who "now has my son's ear . . . and his time in the evening." Although Bonnie's son and daughter-in-law spent Christmas Eve with her and the rest of the family, she said that it "kills her" when they drive down to visit Ashley's family on Christmas. She explained, "I was just a wreck all day. . . . I was heartbroken because my baby wasn't there with me on Christmas." A minute later, though, Bonnie added, "That is how I raised him, to be a partner with his wife and to think of her first. It is the right thing, but I don't have to like it. . . . I would kill him if it were anything less."

Bonnie was proud of the kind of husband that her son was, but regretted the implications that it had for her relationship with him. Bonnie also said that she had to "be aware of the jealousy that she felt so that she did not make things worse [for her relationship with them] or ruin her son's marriage." She later explained that if her daughter-in-law knew how jealous she was, it would create a wedge between them and make everyone uncomfortable about visiting. Also, her son might feel pulled between them if he realized how jealous she felt. Spending more time with his mother might upset his wife, which Bonnie did not want to happen. Bonnie ended this line of discussion by saying, "So I just suck it up. I don't want my problems to affect him and his marriage and I *don't* want things to get worse. Like I said, I don't have to *like it*, though."

While Bonnie and some of the other women felt that they should not express their jealousy over their daughters-in-law, other mothers added that they should not show disappointment in how their relationships with their sons had changed, for the benefit of the relationship. Consider Carol's comment:

> The mother-in-law has to make up her mind that she is not in the marriage. The minister said, "You are now man and wife, not man and wife and mother-in-law. . . ." If you show you are disappointed, you will build tensions and only lose. Besides, if the mother-in-law recognizes the point of marriage, she would not take offense anyway. If [a child] wants the same relationship with their parents as husband or wife, then why would you bother to leave home and get married in the first place? I believe that [my kids'] marriages are not my business. . . . I don't take offense when they put their partner first. . . . If you believe in the bond of marriage and what they are trying to build together for themselves . . . you can't take offense . . . you can't be disappointed. . . . Your son is not "yours" anymore. . . . You might have opinions and questions about what they are doing, but you will have nothing but sorrow if you don't keep them to yourself.

Later she added, "I never made demands. I never let anyone feel that they had to be anywhere or do anything . . . that there were expectations. As a result, they were more likely to come back. At least that is what I think." Like Bonnie, Carol felt that she should not show her disappointment in how her relationship with her son had changed, both because he was right in putting his spouse's needs ahead of her needs and because she felt that being forthcoming about her disappointment would only add to the distance between them.

These and other mothers were clearly torn in recognizing that they felt jealous or disappointed but knowing that they should not express it. Although this was not a longitudinal study, it would be fascinating to see how these relationships develop over time. It would add great insight into the relationship to know whether or not keeping their disappointment to themselves did in fact increase the likelihood of their sons continuing to visit. When the women were asked how they managed to conceal their feelings, they said that they "bit [their] lip a lot" and that they kept in mind what was best for their sons. Several of the women said that they unleashed their feelings to their friends, although their friends did not share their beliefs and were more forthcoming about their own disappointments with their children. The women said that they did not burden the other children with their sadness (although we have only their own perception of this). Some of the women reminded themselves of what it had been like to be a daughter-in-law. A few said that they focused on other things rather than the loss of their children, particularly their sons. Sally said, "Thank God for my husband and my career. I concentrate on them rather than missing my children." Another woman said, "I don't see as much of my children as I would like, but I stay busy with my grandchildren. Some of them can come over on their bikes; the others I go and get. They come anytime. It makes me feel like I am helping them *and* my children when we spend time together." Another mother said that although she does not spend as much time with her sons as she used to, she spends more time with her daughters since they have had children. She said, "My daughters call several times a day, asking what to do about this or that. My sons don't call as much as I would like, but I manage. When they do come, I just enjoy it that much more."

It is interesting to note that according to the quote above, Carol clearly felt that it was no longer her place to have knowledge of her son's personal business. She also stated that "your son is no longer yours [following marriage]." For Carol, allowing her daughter-in-law to be her son's main confidant and recognizing her secondary place in his life were necessary challenges in order to maintain a healthy relationship with a married son.

Overall, most of the women, then, were resigned to the changes in their relationships with their sons. Many actually pulled back on their expectations so as to not be hurt by the change. For example, they did not visit without calling first, accepted (albeit reluctantly) that their sons would spend some holidays with their in-laws, and asked for less assistance from them around the house. Others tried not to "rock the boat" by keeping their thoughts to themselves. One of the women had experienced a significant rift in her relationship with her son. The rift had more to do with the son's personal style, however, as he often offended his mother by his overt directness.

Those women who sought to make changes made only small inroads. Most often they would tell their children that they would like to see them more often. Mothers usually brought this up with their child only, rather than the couple, although they usually expressed a desire to see the daughter-in-law (or son-in-law) too. In these cases, the child would usually visit alone. In only a few cases did mothers-in-law try to see only their child. This suggests that the children-in-law feel more comfortable in not visiting their in-laws than mothers feel in not inviting them. The mothers in this study did not make threats to disinherit their children or otherwise jeopardize their relationships. Such situations have been reported in other studies of mothers-in-law and daughters-in-law.[13]

Several of the women, however, said that they would "do something" (or had done something) if they thought that they were "losing" one of their children. Mary Ann said that she would find out what the problem was and rectify it. She added that if that meant having to approach others in the family about their behavior, then "so be it." In fact, Mary Ann had already taken the initiative to make sure that her children stayed close. For example, she invited each of her children-in-law out to lunch on a monthly basis so that they felt part of the family, held "welcome to the family" parties for her daughters-in-law when her sons married, and worked regular family get-togethers around her children's (and their families) own schedules and tastes. In other words, Mary Ann "managed" the family and its relationships so that all would stay close.

A few of the mothers-in-law handled the change by making jokes with their sons. That is, they used humor to manage their ambivalence. One mother told me that she and her son manage the tension through their shared sense of humor. She said, "I went to visit last summer, and they were all so busy. I said to my son [laughing], 'You call this a visit? If I were dead, then you would have time for a visit. Why wait 'til then?'" Then she added, "There is peace. Peace reigneth."

RISKING ALIENATION

All of the mothers were aware of the social perception of mothers-in-law and daughters-in-law as constantly in battle with one another. They were also keenly aware of the stereotypes of mothers-in-law as controlling and interfering. Most stated that they tried to avoid becoming these stereotypes but walked a fine line of also encouraging their children (especially sons) to visit more. There was some variation in how much they felt they could "impose" without alienating their daughters-in-law. Most commonly, mothers told their sons that they missed them and wanted them to stop by more. This was expressed as often to sons who did not visit as it was to daughters who did not visit. Mothers, however, did not ask to be invited more often to their sons' homes while they did ask to be invited to their daughters' homes. A few said that although they noted an inequity in how much their sons visited their in-laws over them, they did not share this with their sons for risk of alienating their daughters-in-law. Most said that they felt more comfortable going to their daughter's home than their son's home because it was "her home." While they felt less comfortable imposing on their daughter-in-law's home and *her* [emphasis added] family, they felt quite comfortable asking their sons to visit more, with or without the rest of his family.

Mothers were asked if they felt that they were expected to "cut the cord" or "apron strings" more with their sons than with their daughters. They were also asked if there was a perception that their sons should be more independent of them than their daughters. None agreed that they were expected to "cut ties," but a few felt that their sons should be more independent than their daughters. They also felt that there was more distance sometimes between them and their sons versus their daughters. One of the women explained that this was probably more superficial than anything, however. She stated,

> I don't see my son as often as my daughter. He is more independent that way. He doesn't ask my opinion, while she does. He doesn't tell me what is going on, but she does. So on the surface it might look like I have "cut the cord" more with him than with her, but the depth of love is the same [with both children]. That doesn't change just because you get married.

None of the mothers said that they had to "cut the cord" with their sons or risk alienating their daughters-in-law. Instead, their concern for how their daughters-in-law might affect their relationships with their sons was subtler than that. Those who were conscientious of the situation said that they relied less on their sons than they did before they were married and that they did not call their sons in the evenings because that was their sons' time with their families. They did not ask too much of their sons' time because it was now split with their wives and children. Mothers appeared to be less conscientious of impinging on their daughters' time with their husbands but did note the time that they needed to care for their children in the evenings.

THE MOTHER, SON, AND DAUGHTER-IN-LAW TRIAD

What is it about the triad between mother, son, and daughter-in-law that poses such a challenge? Traditionalists would argue that the new wife is taking the place of the mother, but such an argument infantilizes adult men in our society. Nor would I argue that mothers-in-law and daughters-in-law are so dependent on men that they are actually competing for them or battling to control them. However, there are a number of structural factors that challenge the triad of mother, son, and daughter-in-law.

Earlier researchers have examined the factors that lead to difficult relationships between mothers-in-law and daughters-in-law.[14] In-laws lack a shared history that otherwise binds family members. Likewise, in-laws are neither totally in nor out of the family but are thrust into situations where they are expected to treat one another like family and meet all of the obligations of family. Daughters-in-law feel particularly alienated when the boundaries around her husband's family are impermeable and the family does not incorporate her. Likewise, mothers-in-law become resentful if they feel that their daughters-in-law have not bridged the gap between them or included them in their sons' lives. Thus, much of the tension revolves around the creation of a new and separate family. Hostilities tend to remain in situations where the initial separation of families goes poorly. Problems also arise in situations where the families disagree about the acceptable degree of separation from one another.[15]

What about the relationship between the mother and son, though? Results of this research suggest that additional structural factors account for the unique changes in relationships between mothers and their sons following the sons' marriage. In particular, mothers become dissatisfied with the relationship in situations where the couple spends more time with the wife's family than the husband's family following marriage. According to the adult children in this study, couples are only slightly more likely to spend more time with the wife's family than the husband's family.[16] Yet mothers suggest that it happens more frequently than this. According to the mothers, couples tend to spend more time with the wife's family than with the husband's family. This confirms earlier suggestions that men get pulled in to their wife's family more frequently than women get pulled in to their husband's family.[17] In fact, any decrease in time that men spent with their family was experienced negatively by many of the mothers. While mothers did not see this as "losing" their sons, they did believe that it was a lessening of ties, which some mothers resented.

Sons expressed frustration at the conflict between their mothers and wives. One of the sons said, "When my back is to the wall like that . . . caught between them . . . I go red and I just have to leave for a couple of hours." When asked what he meant by his back being to the wall, he said, "It is usually a situation where my mother wants to do one thing and [my wife] wants us to do something else. It is usually about something that really isn't very important, but they are both upset. I get caught in the middle. They both want me to do something, but really, what can I do?" According to one mother, sons usually "take their wives' side" in these situations. She added, "They want to please their wives, so they go along with them." Based on what the sons and daughters said, however, men usually go through several iterations of trying to please both people and do not necessarily always side with their wife. Many daughters-in-law are particularly unhappy about the way that their husband sides with his mother or about his willingness to do what his mother wants, even if it hurts her, the wife.[18]

One husband was so distraught over the conflict between his wife and mother that he was considering divorce. Colin had separated from his wife once before because she did not want his family to be around. He felt that she was being unreasonable and that she did not want her own family around either. Colin and his wife had reconciled after she said that she would include his family more. According to Colin, though, his wife had not kept her promise. Colin wanted to socialize with more people in general but felt that his wife was overly sensitive and never forgave what she thought was an insult. Colin stated, "Something has to give."

SUMMARY AND IMPLICATIONS

While mothers do not feel that they have to "cut ties" with their sons when they marry, they do experience a change in (and often a "lessening" of) the relationship. While daughters stay more connected to the family following leaving home or marrying, sons get pulled in to their wife's family. There is an asymmetry in intergenerational relationships in favor of staying more connected to the wife's side of the family. In fact, mothers will state that it is the wife's mother who is the "primary grandmother." While few adult children believe that they spend more time with the wife's parents than the husband's, mothers are more likely to note a discrepancy in the amount of time their sons spend with them over their wives' families. The decrease in time with a son feels like a loss in the relationship to the mother to varying degrees. Sons get pulled in to their wife's family because their wife and mother-in-law are the primary kin keepers and because husbands are less likely to keep in touch with their parents on their own.[19]

How do mothers handle these changes? Mothers did not feel that it was in their best interest to make demands on their sons and daughters-in-law to see them more. This was in part because they felt that their sons were in the right to spend more time with their wives and that they needed to accept the lessening of ties. As one mother said, "I do not have to like it, though." Mothers did feel that it was in their best interest not to show their disappointment or hurt and to give their sons the room that they needed to spend time with their "own" families. Mothers were less likely to believe that they had to curb their attachments to their daughters for their sons-in-law's sake, suggesting that there is less dissonance in the roles of wife and daughter than in the roles of husband and son. While sons are not expected to "cut the cord" the way that popular perception sometimes suggests, they are more likely than women to feel that they should focus to a greater extent on their own family following marriage. Relationships between mothers and sons were only slightly more likely to worsen following marriage than relationships between mothers and daughters. However, the change appears to be in the degree of closeness between the mother and son, which is partially usurped by the wife and her family. Thus, mothers "lose" their sons to the extent that daughters stay close to their own family.

Earlier researchers have argued that women control men's access to kin.[20] Results of this research suggest that women do indeed affect how much time men spend with kin, but that men still spend some time with family separate from their wife. Mike, in particular, spent a significant amount of time helping his mother around her house. Chris spent time with both his mother and each of his siblings. Still, the presence of a wife may lessen the amount of time that sons spend with their mother as a result of women's ties to their own family being higher for them in their hierarchy of family obligations.

· 8 ·

The Evolution of Intergenerational Relationships Following Children's Marriages

Few studies have focused on how parent–adult child relationships change over time. Those that have, have found that 20 percent of relationships improve over time while 20 percent deteriorate. The remaining 60 percent stay the same.[1] Learned patterns of interaction continue to influence parent-child relations even as grown children move into adult roles, thus creating such stability in relationships.[2] Major life course events, however, create possibilities for changing old patterns. For example, parents report a lessening of conflict and power issues but do not feel as close to their children after they leave home.[3] Likewise, children's marriages lead to less contact with parents and less receipt and provision of emotional, financial, and practical assistance.[4] Other researchers have found though that a daughter's marriage improves relationships with both parents.[5] Divorce and problems in a daughter's marriage later strain parent-child relationships. Likewise, parental divorce and declines in parental health lead to deteriorating relationships.[6] Interestingly, there are few differences between mothers and fathers in the same family regarding continuities and changes in relationships with adult children as they become adults.[7]

Understanding how parent-child relationships change over time is important in and of itself. Most relationships are not completely static but are transformed as people are influenced by their own maturation and progression across the life course, including being influenced by the attaining and relinquishing of new roles and responsibilities. Relationships can also be affected by the simple passage of time and accumulated history. Recognizing how relationships change over time can also inform us of the impact of shared roles and learned patterns of interaction on parent–adult child relationships.

81

Both generational (or cohort) differences as well as time (or period) effects can result in change over time. As such, there are limitations to inferring change by comparing generations. This analysis will explain the evolution of intergenerational relationships by examining older family members' recollections of change over time. However, in order to take advantage of the lucidity of the present day, the chapter will also include younger respondents' (both mothers and adult children) descriptions of the early years in parent–adult child relationships.

THE EARLY YEARS FOLLOWING MARRIAGE

As was discussed in chapter 6, the majority of parents and adult children believed that their relationships with one another had not been affected by the adult child's marriage. Instead, parent–adult child relationships remained quite similar to what they were before marriage. Some of these mothers and children stated that any changes in the relationship had occurred when the child went off to college. They described this change as an increase in the child's independence and the parent and child seeing less of one another rather than any lessening of affection between them. Other mothers, however, stated that the relationship changed very little when the child moved out for the first time or when they married. These families tended to be quite close to one another, to have fewer adult children, and to live in close proximity.

Adult children whose relationships with their parents changed very little with marriage introduced their spouse into the relationship early on while dating. These adult children saw their parents frequently and shared leisure time with them. Boyfriends and girlfriends were included more often in small increments, making the transition a smooth one. Parents continued to spend some time with their child alone and some time with the couple, both before and after they married. These relationships usually did not require long visits, nor did they incur any sudden change. Most of these relationships were quite positive. Parents and adult children shared everyday activities such as shopping and going out to dinner. Other sibling(s) were often included as well.

It was more common for relationships to change to only a small degree following marriage. The mothers in these relationships tended to be very conscientious not to "make things worse" in the relationship by voicing their disappointments. As one mother said, "It would do me no good to let my son know that I feel left out . . . that I am, well, maybe jealous of all of the time that his wife has with him. I am better off by not *creating* [her emphasis] conflict." These mothers primarily noted having less time with their adult children and that their children's best friend/confidante was now their spouse rather than them.

Those relationships that did change significantly tended to worsen and were more likely to be mother-son relationships rather than mother-daughter relationships. Mothers in these relationships tended to believe that they had been significantly "cut off" from their children and that the couple spent more time alone or with the other in-laws than with them. One mother stated, "It must have been part of her plan all along, get the ring on her finger and then pull him over to her side of the family. . . . They spend all of their time with her family. . . . She would love it if he would just forget about us. If my son disagrees, she makes his life miserable. He is in a no-win situation." Other mothers did not necessarily attribute the conflict to their daughters-in-law solely, but they did recognize the tendency for couples to spend more time with the wife's family than with the husband's family. One son said, "I think that my parents realize that I married [wife's name], not them. I want to be a good son, but well, if I have to choose, I choose my wife. Fortunately I don't feel caught in the middle very often, thanks to my wife. My folks are pretty good about it too. They don't ask too much of me . . . except at the holidays."

Adult children whose relationship with their parents worsened following marriage attributed this to either the expected consequences of marriage or the unfortunate behaviors of family members. Vicki, for example, believed that her mother's insistence that her husband attend family events had contributed to her separation from him. While she had felt some tension with her mother before she married (regarding her mother's insistence that she visit more frequently than Vicki wanted to), the tension increased considerably after she married. Vicki felt pulled between her husband, whom she wanted to spend her leisure time with, and her mother, whom she felt obligated to visit. The relationship also worsened because her mother was so disappointed in her choice of husband and his unwillingness to visit with Vicki. Vicki felt that she had to at first make excuses for him and then later defend him to her parents. Vicki explained, "It caused tension between me and my mom. . . . I understood where he was coming from, but she didn't. He is just a loner. [He] did not mind me going alone [to visit her parents], but *my mother* [her italics] minded me going alone. It was stressful to have to make excuses and to listen to her."

Likewise, Colin and his wife had separated at one point in his marriage because he felt that his wife was (inappropriately) unable to get along with both his parents and her own parents. He felt that his wife had cut the couple off from all outside communications. They reconciled after she promised to include his parents more.

Other children believed that the changes in their relationships with their parents were the normal consequences of marriage. Robert, for example, stated that he had to concentrate more on his career and home following marriage in order to provide for his family. Don believed that he needed to turn his focus toward his wife once he married because the Bible stated as much.

A minority of the mothers felt that their relationships with their children actually improved following marriage. One of the mothers stated that her daughter became less self-centered after she married. It was mothers of sons, however, who were more likely to say that their children visited more frequently and became more family oriented after marriage. These mothers were very grateful for the increase in the amount of time that they spent with their sons as a result of their daughters-in-law.

THE MIDDLE YEARS

The second significant change to affect parent–adult child relationships following marriage was the introduction of grandchildren. Mothers of both sons and daughters stated that their children had less time for them once their grandchildren were born. Interestingly, this did not necessarily change as the grandchildren grew older. This may have been the result of patterns of association being established and/or the fact that parents continued to be absorbed with their children even during and after their adolescence. Nevertheless, parents and adult children visited one another more often once grandchildren were born, even though the adult children may have had less time overall for their parents.

Many of the mothers and daughters stated that parenthood brought them closer together. They said that they "shared motherhood." Mothers pointed out that their daughters asked for advice more frequently and that they had more in common to talk about. Daughters appreciated the fact that their mothers helped them out with child care. They wanted their children to know their grandparents and to have a feeling of family. Only a couple of the adult children believed that their children were "better off" without their grandparents.

The introduction of grandchildren also created conflict in the relationship, however. Mothers were frequently unhappy with the way that either their children or children-in-law were raising their grandchildren. Sadie was incensed that her son and daughter-in-law did not keep a kosher kitchen for her grandchildren or provide a calmer environment for her autistic granddaughter. Mary Ann stated that she had to pick her battles over when to "interfere" in her children's disciplining of her grandchildren. Sons and daughters were also acutely aware of the tension that disciplining and raising their children created with their own parents. Sarah explained,

My mother is very old fashioned. I don't like the sexist things that she says around my daughter or the language that she uses. I see my daughter look up every time that my mother swears. . . . I also get defensive about the way that I am raising my children. I know that my mother thinks that they are spoiled and that I should keep them cleaner. My husband and I have different values. . . . My mother has no idea just how busy our lives are. My kids are in all kinds of activities. My mother was never willing to do that for us. So I feel pressured to invite her more. She assumes that we are sitting around twiddling our thumbs, while I am running back and forth to lessons and practices.

Apart from the introduction of grandchildren, relationships between parents and adult children typically did not worsen during the middle years. If anything, relationships improved as each generation adjusted to the changes that accompanied marriage. In-laws grew more accustomed to and accepting of their differences and resigned themselves to the situation at hand. Having less conflict between their spouse and parents enhanced the parent-child relationship as well.

The stabilization of visiting patterns played a large part in improving the bond between parent and child. Parents were not necessarily happy with the frequency of visits, but the visits no longer created the conflict that they once did. One mother offered the following example,

I have just accepted the fact that when my son visits, he is going to be working the whole time. At least we have dinners together, and I can look forward to that. . . . Before, though, I used to turn myself inside-out trying to pull him from his computer. I would be upset the whole time which got my husband upset and then got my son upset. The visit would end with everyone mad at each other.

Another mother said,

It used to really bother me that my daughter and I did not do more mother-and-daughter things together, like going shopping. But my daughter lives three hours away. She is happy, though, in her own life. . . . I just go shopping with my friends instead and see her when I can. . . . Now I notice, though, that my sister-in-law expects my niece to be there [at her house] every weekend. It is really not fair.

Adult children also grew more comfortable with their parents as visits stabilized. Sarah explained,

I just accept now that when my mother visits that she is going to say things in front of my children that I would rather she not. Plus, she is going to

do or say something that makes me feel like I am no more than a little kid
again. But at least it doesn't result in the blow-ups like it used to where I
lose my cool. . . . Plus, she doesn't get upset that I don't invite her more.
. . . So I guess we have finally reached a compromise.

Intergenerational relationships may also improve during the middle years
because it is the time period in which generations are most likely to be independent of one another. Adult children are less likely to need financial assistance
than they were when they were single or first married. Likewise, parents do not
yet need caregiving assistance or help with activities of daily living.[8]

THE LATER YEARS

According to both parents and adult children, parents' infirmities and widowhood challenged their relationships in the later years. The majority of
widowed mothers stated that their children became much more solicitous of
them once their husband died. They consistently described their children as
being caring and concerned about them. Children were more likely to invite
them to dinner and for visits. Children also called more often to check on
their parents. Mothers said that their sons stopped by their home more frequently to fix things for them or to check up on them. Daughters stopped by,
sometimes with their own grandchildren, to visit. One daughter explained,

When my father died, well, I knew that our time with mom was ticking
too. It was the last thing that I could do for dad, looking out for mom.
He would have wanted me to do that. . . . There are a lot of things that I
was surprised that she doesn't know how to do, like balance a checkbook.
. . . I check up on her more because there are things that she doesn't even
know that she doesn't know . . . like you have to change the oil in the car.

Several of the older children said that they had a greater appreciation for
their parents and parents-in-law as they aged. A few of the women said that
their mothers-in-law were more dear to them as they got older, especially
those that had lost their own mothers earlier in life. Sons and daughters also
noted that their parents had had to struggle financially more than they did.
Daughters pointed out that their mothers had fewer opportunities than they
had, especially outside of the home. In some cases, this greater appreciation
tended to counteract any tension that existed earlier in the relationship.

None of the mothers required caregiving from their adult children,
although one mother, who was wheelchair bound, received some assistance
from her daughter in getting outside of her home. Several of the adult chil-

dren, however, noted that parents needed financial assistance or help with home maintenance, yard work, or running errands. Adult children did not believe that providing such assistance had impaired their relationship with their parents; they appeared to accept it as part of their parents' aging. None of the children felt that their parents were being inappropriately dependent, although assisting parents earlier in life might have worsened relationships, particularly if children felt that the assistance was inappropriate for their stage of the life course. Parents, however, were still relatively young. It could be that as impairments grow worse or if dementia sets in, there will be a negative impact on parent–adult child relationships.

Adult children stated that they grew closer to their parents as they aged. They had less to argue about, such as differences in child rearing, and more in common, such as shared life stages. One son said, "I used to be angry with my mother for putting up with the abuse all those years, for not getting us out of it. Now I know though that she was stuck. When you have kids and bills, where are you going to go? . . . I see my own wife. . . . I understand more." Another daughter said, "We have less to argue about now that my kids are grown. . . . Now we are both grandparents. Now I am the one that has to watch what she says. . . . I try to learn how to age gracefully from my mother . . . how to handle retirement and widowhood. I see now that my mother is a strong person. I hope that I can be that when I go through [those things]."

Relationships tended to improve when parents and adult children moved closer to one another. A number of the adult children had moved nearer to either their parents or their parents-in-law after their own children were born. This allowed the generations to spend more time together and for their lives to intersect to a much greater degree. Adult children also hoped to have assistance from their parents with babysitting to augment day care. Only one couple lived with the husband's parents, although this was a short-term arrangement while they were building a house. Several other families shared a duplex or triple-decker or lived on the same street. In comparison, fewer parents moved to be closer to their children when they retired. It was more likely that they visited more often or stayed for a longer period of time in comparison to preretirement. At least according to the parents, this did not result in any conflict. Instead, they felt that they grew closer to their children as a result of sharing a larger part of their lives.

CHANGE ACROSS TIME

What, then, changes in parent–adult child relationships across time? Many relationships start out positively as children become adults and change very little across the life course. However, it is more likely for there to be some change as children marry or leave home. In instances where marriage has a significant negative effect, there is certainly opportunity for the impact of marriage to lessen and for relationships to improve. This was not always the case, however; some parent–adult child relationships remained conflicted over time.

A few of the relationships that were negatively affected by marriage did improve over time. Parents accepted, albeit begrudgingly, the reduced amount of time that they had with their children. They grew more accustomed to visits and visiting schedules even if the sources of conflict during those visits did not change. As one mother said, "I accept it, but I don't have to like it." In-laws did not necessarily work out their differences, but the conflict that resulted was minimized. This allowed for parent-child relationships to improve as well.

Parents and adult children also learned to set aside their differences for the good of others, particularly the grandchildren. Grandparents wanted to spend time with their grandchildren and parents wanted their young children to know their extended family. A few of the daughters-in-law also said that they learned to get along with their in-laws for their husband's sake.

Interestingly, the sources of tension often changed. Earlier in life, parents were sometimes unhappy about their child's choice of spouse or lifestyle. Later that feeling extended to dissatisfaction with the way that they raised their children. Likewise, children sometimes felt a generational divide relative to their parents and were at times resentful of the choices that their parents had made. Although it was not found in this study, the potential exists for caregiving and parental dementia to lead to conflict in later life.[9]

Adult children's time constraints continued to challenge relationships across the life course. They were most acute for daughters when their own children were young and the requirements of their work were high. The increase in visiting and calling when parents were widowed, however, suggests that either time demands lessen or that older adult children put those demands aside when parental needs increase.

Intergenerational relationships also improved as a result of family members' lives intersecting to a greater degree over time. Because of the increase in life expectancy, the potential exists for parents and adult children to share more roles and life stages to a greater degree than ever before. While adult children were quick to point out the ways in which their generation differed from that of their parents, both generations pointed out the benefits of sharing motherhood and grandparenthood. Likewise, adult children looked toward their parents for models of retirement and widowhood.

Life course events also changed intergenerational relationships. For example, widowhood drew adult children to their parents as they sought to provide assistance and as they became more aware of their parents' mortality.

Seeing their parents grow older also tended to soften any prior resentments that they might have had and to counteract the source of any conflict, at least for some adult children.

SUMMARY AND IMPLICATIONS

Thus, both generations experienced change in parent and child bonds over time. While some relationships remained unaltered after marriage, most did not. The greatest changes following marriage occurred after grandchildren were born, although the changes occurred in multiple ways that sometimes cancelled one another out. The second greatest change occurred as parents aged. Although parents did not always need more care, children became more solicitous anyway. Episodes of expressed conflict tended to lessen, although the sources of conflict did not necessarily change.

Earlier research suggested that learned patterns of interaction continue to influence parent-child relationships as grown children move into adult roles but that major life course events create possibilities for changing those patterns.[10] Results of this research support these findings. Problems could not always be resolved, and parents remained frustrated by the lack of time that they had with their adult children as well as other sources of conflict. Ambivalence often continued for decades after adult children married. Earlier patterns of visiting and calling usually did not change, although family members learned to accept the conflict that resulted. Widowhood, however, was an important life course change that resulted in adult children becoming more solicitous of their elderly parents.

Results of this analysis also suggest support for intergenerational role similarity theory. This theory argues that when grown children move into adult roles their roles and experiences become similar to that of their parents, which strengthens their relationships.[11] Mothers, in particular, believed quite strongly that shared motherhood had improved their ties with their daughters. Likewise, conflict lessened as adult children became more understanding of the choices that their parents had made in life. Still, it was important to adult children to point out the ways in which their generation differed from that of their parents.

Parent–adult child relationships are not necessarily fixed after marriage. Instead they have the potential for change and growth. Chapter 10 includes the advice that mothers offered to other parents for maintaining close relationships with adult children over the life course. The next chapter looks at the effects of divorce on parent–adult child relationships.

· 9 ·

Divorce and Later-Life Families

$\mathcal{L}$ike marriage, divorce is an important life course event that affects inter-generational ties. This includes the adult child's divorce as well as the parents' divorce. Previous research has shown that parental divorce leads to deterio-rating intergenerational ties.[1] Relationships with fathers and divorced parents have the weakest levels of intergenerational cohesion.[2] Divorce undermines ties with both mothers and fathers suggesting that the cause of the weakening ties extends beyond custody arrangements that usually favor the mother. This chapter will explore the impact of parental divorce further. It will examine, for example, the effect of the child's relationship with the stepparent on the parent-child bond as well as other factors related to parental divorce.

Adult children's divorce also affects intergenerational ties. However, this effect is mediated by gender. A daughter's divorce leads to strained intergen-erational ties with both mothers and fathers. However, a son's divorce leads to deteriorating relationships with fathers only. Neither marital problems nor divorce hurts the mother-son relationship.[3] More recently researchers have differentiated the disparity between divorced and never-married versus mar-ried children. They found that divorced children are more involved with par-ents than married children on most counts. However, divorced children are less involved with parents than never-married children. This pattern exists for both married men and married women. The authors conclude that marriage substantially restricts relationships with parents for both men and women.[4]

Children's marital status also affects instrumental exchange. Again, the effect is mediated by gender. Divorced sons receive and provide less help than married sons. In contrast, divorced daughters receive *more* help from parents than married daughters. It would appear that grandparents provide more help to whichever family structure includes the grandchildren, especially if there is only one parent available. Divorce does not, however, decrease a daughter's help to parents as it does a son's help.[5] This may be the result of both the need to reciprocate and daughters' closer relationship with parents.

THE EFFECT OF PARENTAL DIVORCE

A minority of the mothers were divorced and/or remarried. Dawn, who had been divorced since her children were quite young, stated that it had not affected her relationship with them. However, she spoke frequently of being jealous of her four children's relationships with their spouses. Several times she made the statement, "He is not my baby anymore," with regard to her sons. Dawn said that she cried all day on Christmas the first year that her son went to his in-law's home for the holiday. It could be that Dawn would be as despondent over her children's independence even if she were married. However, other mothers stated that having a spouse or career helped them to adjust to their children's independence because it gave them something else on which to focus. Susan, for example, stated,

> Thank God for my husband and career. My work . . . I can really sink my teeth into it and focus on it. If I had a nine-to-five [job], it wouldn't be the same. . . . Stuart and I have more time for each other now too. We have reconnected in important ways. When your kids are young, you are both so zapped from their needs. It is not just that we have more energy to focus on each other, but there is nothing in the way anymore of being together.

Despite her divorce, Dawn and her children created a strong sense of family unity among themselves. She spoke frequently of family get-togethers and holidays and referred to her family as "the Smith gang." All of her children lived nearby, and she felt close to all four of them. She believed that they were close to one another as well.

In contrast to her close relationship with her children, Dawn said that her children do not have contact with their father. In fact, several comments suggested that her children did not know where their father was. Dawn stated that her ex-husband had been living in other parts of the country since he abandoned the family twenty years ago. It did not appear that he had paid child support over the years.

Joan divorced when her oldest son was an adolescent and her fraternal twins were preschoolers. She stated that she had a closer relationship with her older son than her younger children, including her only daughter, although she would rely on her younger son for emotional support if she needed it.

Joan said that her older son "stepped into his father's shoes" when he left. She believed that this resulted in him being more stalwart than her younger children, but that it also resulted in him being more likely to "check" on her and to call her frequently. Joan's children saw their father infrequently although they did have something of a relationship with him. She said that she had been very careful not to "poison" her children against their father and stepmother.

Joan conscientiously waited to remarry until after her children had left home. She explained, "We waited until the twins had their own apartments. I just did not want to disrupt the family home. I did not want them to have to wake up and have to deal with Peter being here . . . to a stepfather in their home. . . . Things are comfortable between Peter and my children and between me and his children."

Liz had two grown children, one son and one daughter. She divorced while her daughter was a teenager and her son was an adolescent. Although she was still more intimate with her daughter than her son, she stated that she was closer to her son than most mothers and sons. Liz said that her son called frequently to see how she was and to ask if there was anything that he could do for her. When he was in college, they would talk for hours when he got home, sometimes in the middle of the night. At the time of the interview, Liz's son still talked to her if something was bothering him, even if it was about his wife. Liz said that she tried to give both sets of children and their spouses plenty of space and to respect their privacy.

Liz said that both of her children were close to their father, although her daughter was closer to him than her son. She explained, "It may be because of the mother and son thing or it may be because [my son] doesn't remember his father, well, living with us anyway . . . that he is closer to me. My daughter was always Daddy's girl. She and I have always been very close, though." Liz said that she did not think that her children ever felt torn between their two parents. She did think, though, that there was a period when her daughter blamed her for the divorce and that her daughter's teenage years were more difficult as a result of that. The children spent part of the holidays with their father, but Liz believed that they saw her home as the "home base."

Thus, most of the mothers felt that their own relationship with their children had not been hurt by their divorce. If anything, most of the mothers felt that they were closer to their children, particularly their sons, as a result of the divorce. Sons were much more solicitous of their mother's well-being if they were divorced and tended to be emotionally closer. One of the mothers may have had difficulty separating from her married children as a result of the divorce, but other mothers felt that being married and having a career gave them an alternative outlet when their children left home.

According to the mothers, divorce did affect their children's relationships with their father. The level of closeness between adult children and their father varied considerably depending on the father's attempted maintenance of the relationship and geographic proximity. However, most of the children had some kind of relationship with their father. Only a few, however, appeared to have a relationship with their father that approximated the closeness of their relationship with their mother. All of the children had stayed in the maternal home after divorce.

Interestingly, the adult men who were willing to be interviewed were more likely to have divorced parents than the adult women. Still, it was a minority of adult children that had divorced parents. Ed was very angry with his father, but more because he had been abusive to Ed as a child than as a result of the divorce. Ed said several times, "I have scars both on the inside and on the outside." He said that the first time that he stopped being afraid of his father was when he lay dying in a hospital bed. That was a significant turning point in Ed's life. He said that it was only then that he started to love his father.

Ed was proud of the fact that he "takes care" of his mother, Mrs. Ryder. He provided her with an apartment that he owned. He and his wife also provided Mrs. Ryder with any assistance that she needed, such as going to doctors' appointments. Ed said that it was his responsibility because he is the only one of the children that lived in the area. Ed did not describe his relationship with his mother as being close, even though they talked on the phone several times a day. He and his wife counted on his mother to help with babysitting their two sons. Ed said that for a while he was angry with his mother for not leaving his father earlier but that he understood better why she had not been able to do that now that he was married himself.

In contrast, Mike saw his father once a week but his mother only once a year. This was in part due to the fact that she lived on the other side of the country but also to the fact that his wife and mother did not get along. Mike also called his mother much less often than his father. When asked if the quality of his relationships with his parents had anything to do with their divorce, he explained, "Only indirectly. My wife thinks so. . . . I was the oldest son, the one my mother always turned to. She wasn't able to let go [when I got married], and I had to think about my own family. We lived with my mother when I was growing up. Now I see that it would have been better for me to have a father in the house. Children need a father." Mike also felt that his mother was angry with him for being close to his father. He said, "It has always been a tug of war over us kids . . . who we are going to live with, taking sides, holidays. It is a competition for my mother. I think I am more like my father. My wife says that bothers my mother too. I don't know. I don't really think about it either way."

Chris's parents divorced while he was a teenager. He said that he saw his father every couple of years but that he saw his mother more like once a week. Chris said that he felt no animosity toward his father but that they were not particularly close. He explained that they "each had their own families." Chris said that his relationship with his mother was like any other mother-and-son relationship. However, it was noted that Chris continued to fix things around his mother's house for her, even though she had been remarried for several years. He said, "I guess she just got in the habit of asking me to do it. I don't mind really."

Tim also saw his father much less often than his mother. His parents had been divorced since Tim was a toddler. His mother remarried but was recently divorced again. Tim said that he did not see much of his father growing up and that his stepfather had been more of a father figure. However, he said that he was amazed by how much he and his biological father had in common. He explained, "Yes, my parents' divorce certainly affected my relationship with my father back then, when I was a kid. Why dwell on the past, though? Family is family no [matter] what. It is in the blood."

Tim was more cognizant of the effect of his mother's second divorce on his relationship with her and his stepfather. He explained, "I have to help my mother more now that my stepfather isn't there. She does a lot of it herself, but it is an old house. Plus she can't fix anything herself to save her life. . . . My stepfather keeps to himself now. . . . I don't know why. . . . We try calling."

Amy saw her father rarely since her parents divorced. She attributed this to her stepmother, though, and not her father. She said, "One time I went to my father's house. There had been a guy who had been stalking me. I was in the area of my father's, so I drove to his house. I was out on the lawn screaming for him, threatening to kill myself. He never came out. After that, I was forbidden to go there [by my stepmother]. How do you like that?" In describing their more recent relationship, she said, "It is extremely awkward. I am still forbidden to go there. He is sick; he cannot leave the house. The last time that I was there, he had called me and my sister to give us money that my grandmother left us. It was just awful. I can't even call . . . it is forbidden. . . . She [my stepmother] got a restraining order against me. How do you like that?"

Amy was not close to her mother growing up either. She ran away when she was thirteen years old and lived with her aunt. However, she blamed her estrangement from her mother on her mother's alcoholism and not on her parents' divorce. At the time of the interview, Amy's mother had passed away.

In contrast, Sasha continued to have a positive relationship with both of her parents after they divorced. Although she called her father and visited him less frequently than her mother, she said that she still was still close to him. In fact, she said that she spent more holiday time with her father than her mother because her father was "big on holidays." However, she pointed out that having divorced parents meant that she and her husband were "torn three ways" on the holidays. When asked to describe her relationship with her father, she stated,

> My dad and I have a very healthy and normal relationship. He is very doting and caring. He is more of a parent [than my mother]. I don't get along with his wife, but I play the game and do what I can to make him happy. There used to be overt hostility, but there is not so much anymore. . . . I wish that we lived closer. We respect each other. He can be childish, though. . . . He worries, so I don't tell him too much.

In contrast, Amber felt that she had to "play the parent role" with her mother, which she resented. She explained, "My mom and I are very close, but we are more like friends than mother and daughter. I mind it, but I have accepted it." Amber was particularly frustrated with her mother for dating a married man. She felt that some of the problems with her mother probably would not have come up if her parents were still married, but that her mother's main "deficiencies" would still be there. Thus, there would be problems in the relationship even if her parents were still married.

WHEN ADULT CHILDREN DIVORCE

Because of generational differences in divorce rates, mothers were more likely to have at least one divorced child than to have divorced themselves. According to the mothers, they worried more about their divorced children (and any related grandchildren) than their married or single children, which impacted their relationship with them. Several of the mothers also said that they helped their divorced children more than their married children. Mothers were particularly upset with sons who divorced if it resulted in their moving back home or if their son's behavior was responsible for the divorce. This is consistent with previous findings that children's inability to reach normative adult statuses increases ambivalence for mothers.[6]

Betty's youngest daughter was divorced. She said that although the divorce did not make her any more or less close to this daughter, it did result in her helping her daughter more. She explained, "I do more for her than my other two children because she is divorced. I take her son more because he doesn't have a good relationship with his father. I want him to have that family feeling. I give her more financial help. I don't feel any closer to her though." It was particularly important to Betty that the extra assistance that she gave to her divorced daughter did not impact her relationships with her two married children. She added, "I talked to my son about how I do more for my younger daughter and her son. He said, 'Everything you do for them is fine with me. I have a good job.' So there is no jealousy there. My older daughter is fine with it too. She is actually glad that I help her sister out."

Mary Ann said that she was more worried about her oldest daughter, Kathy, who was divorced, than she was about her younger three children. Kathy was trying to regain custody of her children, which Mary Ann supported. She had offered to loan Kathy money to pay for lawyers' fees, but she did not want just to give Kathy the money. She said, "Well, it is not like we have a lot of extra to give away, plus it would not be fair to the other three children and their spouses to give to just one." Mary Ann said that Kathy would probably move to be near her children if she could not get custody of them. Mary Ann was concerned that Kathy would not have a support network in another part of the country. She said that she had to be careful not to get too drawn in to Kathy's problems or they could overwhelm her.

Barbara was very distraught with her divorced son, Chip. She stated, "Chip has always been in trouble. He lives here with me now. He hasn't worked in ten years. He drinks and does drugs. He has been in trouble with the law. . . . He is emotionally immature. His divorce was his downfall. His ex-wife kept moving and moving the kids further away. We are close, but it is tense because of his personality. He cannot get along with anyone. I have to watch what I say." For Barbara, then, her son's divorce affected her relationship with him by causing him to turn to drugs and alcohol. As Barbara was quick to point out, though, Chip had emotional problems even before he divorced. His divorce exacerbated those problems and made him dependent on his mother. Despite the tension in their relationship, Barbara still felt close to her son. Theirs was a highly ambivalent relationship.

Mimi's oldest son, Johnny, had been married and divorced three times. She had not seen him in over a year. Mimi said that her son's marriages did not distance him from her but his divorces did. Johnny removed himself from the family each time that he started having problems in his marriage. Mimi said that she could not justify Johnny's first divorce because he then married the family babysitter. Mimi said, "As a mother, I just couldn't justify it. He distanced himself for that but later apologized and said that he was sorry he had done that." Johnny and his second wife moved into Mimi's basement. Mimi said that she catered to him during that period. She added, "It doesn't stop [i.e., taking care of him] just because he is married." Johnny and his second wife had two children together. Johnny told his mother that he could not afford to live on his own because of his alimony and child support payment to his first wife. Mimi also liked Johnny's third wife; however, he again distanced himself when they had marital problems. Mimi said that her third daughter-in-law came to her after Johnny had beaten her. Johnny denied it, but Mimi said that she "saw the living proof." Mimi had not seen Johnny since his latest divorce, but she was still close to his first and third wives. Mimi believed that Johnny would come around again when he remarried and would resume a place in the family. Mimi's disappointment in her son was not due to his divorces but to the behaviors that accompanied his divorces.

A minority of the daughters but none of the sons who were interviewed had been divorced. Vicki attributed her divorce in part to her mother's insistence that her husband be more a part of the family. She also believed that her divorce had affected her relationship with her parents. She elaborated, saying,

> Now that I am divorced, my parents want to pay for everything for me. I know that my mother looks down on me because I do not make more money. . . . I just bought a condo. My parents have insisted on paying for the down payment even though I have been saving for it. Now my mother needs to know every little thing that I do . . . since the divorce. She wants me there all the time. . . . I feel like I am being smothered.

For Vicki, then, her new divorced status had increased the tension between her and her parents.

Cindy, in contrast, had avoided her mother since she divorced seven years ago. She explained,

> I see my mother or call her about once a month. I am hiding. I don't really like to talk to her. I am afraid that she is going to ask me questions, even though she doesn't. I feel guilty about being divorced, like I disappointed her. I love my mother, but I was closer to my dad. [But] my mother and sister are like best friends. They call each other every day. . . . My brothers are on my mother like glue. None of the others [i.e., other siblings] are divorced.

Judy was divorced for fifteen years before she remarried. She believed that her divorce did not affect her relationship with her parents, but her parents' prejudice toward her second husband's race had impacted it. Judy stated that her new husband was not allowed in her parents' home. However, Judy stayed close to her family despite this. In fact, she lived on the second floor of the house that her parents owned, although she planned to move because of the uncomfortable situation surrounding her new husband. Her parents lived on the first floor, and her married son lived on the third floor. Judy said that her parents did not seem surprised or disappointed when she divorced because other family members had divorced as well. Judy, however, did not live in the same triple-decker as her parents before she divorced. Her divorce, then, had affected her relationship with her parents to the extent that it made her much more physically proximate to them than she was when she was first married. Judy said that she stopped to see her mother for coffee every morning before she went to work. She did not see her father more than once a month, though, because they had conflicting work schedules.

Katie was the only divorced child who grew closer to her parents after her divorce. At the time of the interview, Katie had been divorced for four and a half years. She had decided that she wanted to move closer to her parents, who lived three hours away. She explained, "I met my [ex-] husband when I moved here. He is still here and his parents are still here, but I want my daughter to know her grandparents.[7] I go to visit [my parents] a lot more since we broke up. We are very close. I would like to move home to have a sense of family . . . and so that my parents can know their granddaughter."

SUMMARY AND CONCLUSION

Divorce has multiple effects on intergenerational relationships. Parents' divorce appears to make mothers closer to their children, especially their sons. According to the adult children, it also makes mothers more dependent on them, which can affect their marriage and lead to marital problems. In the long run, then, parental divorce can worsen mother-and-child relationships. Likewise, parental divorce can create tension and distance with the father, although to varying degrees, over both the short and long term. Adult children's relationships with divorced parents are also affected by the attitude of the stepparent and the child's relationship with him or her as well as the age of the child at the time of the divorce. Although rare, it is possible for adult children to have continued close relationships with both parents following divorce.

Mothers tend to worry more about their divorced children than their married or single children. They are also disappointed with sons if their divorce results in them moving home or if they feel that their son's behavior caused the divorce. Overall, divorced daughters experience increased tension with their parents and assume that they have disappointed their parents. Divorce can also cause both sons and daughters to be more financially dependent on their parents, which leads to increased ambivalence and tension in the relationship. This is consistent with previous findings that divorced daughters receive more help from parents than married daughters.[8]

Thus, adult children's divorce appears to compromise intergenerational relationships overall. While a daughter's marriage does not appear to weaken the parent-child bond, divorce does by making daughters more dependent. To some extent, it can alter the closeness of the relationship if children feel that they have disappointed their parents or if mothers must step back from the relationship to avoid being overwhelmed by worrying. In contrast to earlier findings,[9] a divorced son can have poorer relationships with his mother than married or single sons if the divorce increases his dependency on her or if it leads to the son's delinquency and loss of age-appropriate statuses.

· *10* ·

Advice to Mothers for Maintaining Intergenerational Relationships

*M*others were eager to share their experiences and to offer advice to other mothers on how to maintain positive relationships with adult children after they married. Interestingly, the adult children did not offer much advice to one another, since they saw the relationship, and therefore any efforts to improve it, as in the hands of their parents. The nine most common pieces of advice that mothers offered fell within the following five broad categories: allowing the couple to be independent, respecting the couple's marriage, being easy to get along with, creating a sense of family, and having alternative sources of identity in later life. The mothers' advice pertained to maintaining relationships with both sons and daughters. However, it is skewed in the direction of how to get along with daughters-in-law. This suggests that the mothers see getting along with their daughters-in-law as a critical component to maintaining a good relationship with their sons. Their advice follows.

ALLOWING THE COUPLE TO BE INDEPENDENT

Allowing the couple to be independent included letting the couple make their own decisions, not interfering in the relationship (or as the mothers put it, "Don't butt in!"), and waiting for children to visit them when they were busy rather than going to their children's homes.

Let Them Make Their Own Decisions

Many of the mothers believed that you should allow your married children to make their own decisions along with their spouses. Jean has three married children. Her son from a previous marriage was the first to marry. Jean explained that she encouraged all three of her children to be independent and to make their own decisions with their spouse once they were married. She believed that this allowed her to have a better relationship with her children and children-in-law. She said, "I think that my son was worried that I was going to be a controlling mother-in-law. I beat him to the punch line. I told him that I expected them to make their own decisions and that was fine with me. I feel secure that all three kids know right from wrong. So I don't feel bad about them growing up and making their own decisions." Jean added that she sometimes had to explain comments that she made to her daughter-in-law so that she did not offend her or so that she did not seem to be criticizing her daughter-in-law's decisions. For example, she explained,

> When they got married, I told [my daughter-in-law] that I was surprised that one of her brothers wasn't going to walk her down the aisle. She took that as a criticism and got upset. [My son] called me about it, and I explained. Then he explained it to her. I just kept telling them all the time not to worry about what I think and to do things the way that they want. For example, they have a lot of pets and so a lot of fur in the house. I tell them though, "Don't worry about me. Keep your house the way that you want."

Jean believed that this approach had a very positive effect on her relationship with both her son and her daughter-in-law. She said, "Our family is very close. I am very close to my daughters-in-law too. They tell me things that other mothers-in-law would not know. I value their independence and respect them as a family, which makes me more endearing to them. I think that other mothers-in-law would be jealous of my relationship with [my daughters-in-law]."

Likewise, Sue explained,

> I do not ask questions. I do not need to know their business. I do not have any business being in their marriage. That is for them. I might give my advice on practical things if I am asked, but that is as far as it goes. . . . I don't need to know. . . . The gospel says that you leave your mother and father and cling to your husband or wife. I truly believe that. So I bend backwards and look the other way.

"Don't Butt In!"

Many of the mothers also echoed a similar variant of "let them make their own decisions" when they said that mothers (-in-law) should not "butt in."

Marcia explained it succinctly when she said, "I bend over backwards not to butt in to my kids' relationships. I think that is the key to keeping a good relationship [with them]. I don't give unsolicited advice. They are grown-ups now."

"Not butting in" was particularly important when it came to how grand-children were raised. Mary Ann shared the following, "You have to decide if and how many comments you are going to make about the way that the child-in-law disciplines your grandchild or how they treat your child. The other day, I did not say anything but it was clear from my expression that I did not like how my son-in-law was disciplining my grandchild. I was told by my *child* [her emphasis] that it wasn't my issue." Bonnie also said that she did not "mess" with the way that her children-in-law raised her grandchildren as long as they were willing to baptize them.

Letting go of old roles and behaviors was an important part of not butt-ing in. Janice, for example, said that she had "backed off on being bossy in that relationship" because she was no longer "the woman in [her son's] life." She added later, "I learned quickly that his wife is the woman in his life now. She said that I cannot baby him anymore. For example, she does not want me to iron his shirts because she thinks that he should do it for himself. I don't do it anymore because it caused an argument between them."

"I Let Them Come to Me."

Several of the mothers believed that their children would be more likely to want to see them if they did not pressure them to do so. Jean's son was in the army at the time of the interview and had been away frequently during the last two years. Her strategy then was to wait for her son to come to her when he was home. She explained, "My son is away for so long . . . that I don't want to interrupt his time with his family when he first gets home. I just wait for him to come to me. That way . . . he and his wife won't be resentful and I won't feel like I am intruding."

Similarly, Phyllis gave the following advice, "You hold your children tight when they are young. When they are grown, you hold them in the palm of your hand. That way, they want to come back."

RESPECTING THE COUPLE'S MARRIAGE

Many of the mothers felt that they needed to be respectful of the couple's marriage. This included having what one mother referred to as "the right attitude" and, as part of that, including the children-in-law in your family.

"You Need to Have the Right Attitude about Their Marriage."

According to Joan, having the right attitude meant being satisfied to be on the "periphery" of each of her children's families. She said that she did not get upset if her children spent more time with their in-laws, because her "needs [were] being met." Joan had three sons and one daughter. She was close to all three of her daughters-in-law and her son-in-law, but she was particularly close to one of the daughters-in-law. Joan felt welcome in all of their homes, but she always called before visiting. She believed that it was because of her willingness to be on the periphery that there was no tension.

Sally thought that having the right attitude toward your children's marriages was to expect them to be independent and not to be disappointed if they were. She said, "We feel strongly that you bring your children up to be independent and have their own lives. You bring them up to go out on their own. They might or might not choose to have a family. That is up to them. They should be independent though. That is how it should be. They should have their own holidays and family customs and their own core family."

Sue felt equally strongly that the mother needs to stay out of her son's marriage. She stated "I believe that [my kids'] marriages are not my business. . . . I don't take offense when they put their partner first." Likewise, Roseanne said, "I always told my children to put their mates first. I always told them, "Your husband or your wife first and *then* [her emphasis] your parents. I feel very strongly about that."

Some of the mothers pointed out that because children are so busy, it is up to the parents to "fit into the openings in their lives." Many of the mothers also pointed out that they respected their children's privacy. Patty explained, "I don't ever drop in or go over during their family time. I understand that. Their time for their families is theirs. I totally believe in that." She also added, "I don't feel any competition [with the other in-laws]. . . . I don't feel threatened. I know [that] they have another family."

"Include Your (Daughter-)In-Law and be Nice (to Her)."

Many of the mothers-in-law made a point of including their children-in-law in the family from the start. It seemed particularly important to them to include their daughters-in-law. Marcia reminisced,

> [My relationship with my daughter-in-law] is phenomenal. [My son] had never brought anyone home before. He told me, "Mom, there is someone that I would like you to meet. She is very special to me." So I had them come over for dinner. I was nervous. She was the sweetest girl, though.

I liked her right off the bat. I bent over backwards to include her and to be nice to her. One time she and I were talking, and my son was reading the paper. He looked up and smiled and went back to reading his paper. I could tell that he was pleased that she could be so comfortable at our house.

When asked why it is so important to her to include her daughter-in-law, Marcia explained, "I did it because I thought it would be the best way to start a relationship with a daughter-in-law, to get along." Later Marcia added, "I thought that I would have an easier time staying close to my children and us all being a family if I got along with their spouses."

However, Marcia pointed out that not all children-in-law want to be included in the family right away. She tried the same tactics that she used with her daughter-in-law with her future son-in-law. After her son-in-law declined to visit several times, she asked her daughter why he did not come over to visit. Her daughter told her to "back off" and that he was shy. Eventually Matt did start to spend time with the family once Marcia stopped putting pressure on him. She stated, "We had to learn to accept what he could give at the time."

Mary Ann also added, "I am very sensitive to maintaining a good relationship with my children-in-law. I treat them equally to my children, especially on holidays and birthdays." Mary Ann gave each of her daughters-in-law a "welcome to the family" party when they became engaged to her sons. She frequently has lunch with each of her children-in-law separately to maintain a good relationship.

Sadie thought that it was important to get along with her daughter-in-law even if she did not like her. When asked about her relationships with her daughters-in-law, over and over again she would say, "Live and let live." Later she added, "[My son] married a very, very strange girl. She makes weird decisions in their life, and he goes along. My other daughter-in-law is chatty, but she is basically okay. This one though is cold and self-centered. There is no evil or maliciousness, though. . . . I just say, 'live and let live.'"

BEING EASY TO GET ALONG WITH

Mothers recognized that they would have better relationships with their children if they made visiting and the holidays easier for them to juggle. This included recognizing that their children had in-laws to visit as well as visiting them. It also included keeping any dissatisfaction they had about visiting from their children and children-in-law.

Make Holidays and Visits Easy

Patty has two children, both of whom have in-laws that live farther away. Patty said that she "contained" any problems that she might have with her children and their spouses by "not lay[ing] on expectations." For example, on the holidays Patty's children each traveled to their in-laws and stayed for several days. Therefore Patty had a family holiday with her children either before or after they visited their in-laws and at the convenience of the children and children-in-law. Patty said that it was fine with her as long as it worked out best for them.

Similarly, Sue said, "The success of my situation is due to making myself pliable. If Mary wanted to be with her family on Christmas, because many girls do, I would meet them for dessert. I do not take offense. Marriage is like a garden; I do not need to put any weeds in it." Another mother added, "I never make demands. I never let anyone feel that they had to be anywhere or had to do anything. . . . I let them know that I wasn't taking any offense." Other mothers thought that the couples should split the holidays evenly between the two sets of in-laws. JoAnn said that she maintained good relationships with her children and their families by not staying too long when she visited. She explained, "I believe that visiting family is like having fish. You don't want to stay too long."

Phyllis pointed out that she did not press her children to be around on holidays because she had resented it when her own in-laws did so. She reminisced, "I am more relaxed about it [visiting on holidays]. My in-laws always expected us to be there for every holiday. Holidays were like a scene out of *The Godfather* with everyone yelling and the pasta boiling over. We have Christmas the Sunday before at someone's house for the extended family. Then our family has Christmas Eve together. Other than that, though, people come if they can. Hopefully they can and want to."

Keep Your Dissatisfaction under Wraps

Many of the mothers argued that if they were dissatisfied with their relationships with their children or resentful of their children-in-law, it was in their best interest to keep it to themselves. For example, Bonnie said, "If the mother-in-law is not aware of the jealousy [toward her in-law], it can ruin a marriage. I know that I have to be aware of it and not make things worse."

In addition to keeping their dissatisfaction under wraps, mothers also tried to keep their conversations with their children interesting to them in order to maintain their relationship. Sue said, "I realized at one point that I was always telling them about who died or who was sick. I decided that I did not want to do that. [My son] was always in sports, so we talk about sports.

. . . My daughter, we talk about her work and kids." Sue said that it also helps to "pull back" if your children need more time for their own families. For example, her daughter is now very busy with triplets. She said, "I was the one who had to pull back. I carry more on my own."

CREATING A SENSE OF FAMILY

Encourage a Close-Knit Family All Along

Several of the mothers felt that they were able to stay close to their children after they married because they had always taught them to stay close. Patty incorporated boyfriends and girlfriends into the family when they came into the picture as well. She explained,

> We were always a very close-knit family. We always did things together. We never separated ourselves from the kids. We were always behind them. I did not want to lose either of my children, so I included the boyfriend and girlfriend right from the beginning. They were incorporated into the family right from the start. I just felt like the family got bigger. We went from four to eight. The spouses were already a part of the family before they got married. The only thing that changed was that they had a ring on their finger.

Betty believed that her children stayed close to her because she had stayed close to her parents and parents-in-law when the children were growing up. She said, "[They] saw me being close to my family and making sure they saw their father's family. Now they do the same." Likewise, Diane said, "Modeling is the key. Family was always a high priority. We always did things together and that will continue. We always gave them the message that we expected them to stay involved. Part of what makes that easy is that we all get along."

HAVING ALTERNATIVE
SOURCES OF IDENTITY IN LATER LIFE

"You Need to Have Your Own Life!"

Mothers whose children lived a long distance away believed that they needed other avenues to occupy their time once their children were married. Sally felt that women should concentrate on other aspects of their lives when their children leave so that they do not feel bereft. For Sally, her husband and her career made all of the difference in being able to negotiate the changes in her relationships with her children. She felt that by having other things to focus on, she was not as dependent on her adult children. Likewise, Pat said,

> It behooves us [mothers] to understand what is going on and [to] make the best of it. It is your job to make room for the way that the relationship has changed. Mothers who are too close to the son may feel abandoned. You can never get all of your emotional needs met by your children, though. If the mother has her own life, she can be happy for her son and encourage the relationship.

Later, Pat added:

> Your son's main focus isn't you anymore, even if it was before. Your son's main focus should be his wife when he marries. If there is a conflict, he should support his wife. If the mother is smart, she will accept that. The mother needs a balanced life of her own. . . . I have never felt slighted or left out. I just accept it. I get as much attention as I need in a healthy sort of way.

A CAVEAT

It should be pointed out that mothers did not always choose to keep their concerns to themselves, as was exemplified by the examples throughout the book. However, according to the mothers that I interviewed, their advice fell along the lines of respecting the couple's marriage and allowing their children to be independent by keeping their opinions to themselves. While scholars and professionals may choose to advise in another way, this was the opinion of the mothers. Likewise, it may be possible for mothers to find ways to *offer* their advice while still respecting the couple's marriage and their independence.

SUMMARY AND IMPLICATIONS

Mothers' advice to other parents on how to maintain good relationships with their adult children following marriage fell under five main categories: allowing the couple to be independent, respecting the couple's marriage, being easy to get along with, creating a sense of family, and having alternative sources of identity in later life. The first piece of advice, allowing the couple to be independent, reflected the mothers' recognition of the need to "step back" and allow for the formation of a new nuclear family. This included understanding that the couple needed to do things their own way, such as raising their children as they saw fit, and that they needed to have their own time together and create their own family rituals. It also suggested recognition of the couple's autonomy.

The second piece of advice, respecting the couple's marriage, indicates another set of understandings. It suggests that at least some mothers recognize that their children's personal information will no longer be known to them after they marry and that their children's marriages are private and separate from them. Underlying this is a deeper acknowledgment of their children's autonomy once they are married. It further suggests that mothers want children to be able to care for themselves and to make wise decisions and understand that their children are no longer "theirs" exclusively. The third piece of advice, being easy to get along with, demonstrates recognition that maintaining a relationship with their children requires getting along with their children-in-law; that is, that their children's marriages will have an impact on their relationships with them. It also suggests an appreciation for children-in-law being part of the extended family. Mothers also seemed to realize that their children had another family, their in-laws, of which they were a part and that their holiday time was now compressed.

The last pieces of advice focused on positive actions that mothers can take, such as creating a sense of family when children are still young. Encouraging other mothers to have an alternative source of identity in later life reveals their understanding that their married children can no longer be the center of their lives. As one mother put it, "You can't be *too* [her emphasis] caring anymore. It would seem like you were overbearing. My daughter really wouldn't like it. . . . She has her husband now."

· 11 ·

Reciprocal Effects

How Do Intergenerational Relationships Impact Adult Children's Marriages?

So far we have examined the impact adult children's marriage has on their relationship with their parents. Before turning to the conclusions, this chapter will consider the potential for reciprocal effects, that is, the impact of intergenerational relationships on adult children's marriages and intimate relationships. This chapter will focus on the responses of the adult children in the sample.

Previous research has shown that relationships between parents and adult children can impact children's marriages, but most recent studies of *divorce* do not consider the effect of parent–adult child relationships on the potential for divorce.[1] Studies of daughters-in-law do cite rare instances in which women's problems with their mother-in-law have harmed their marriage to the point of considering divorce;[2] however, most daughters-in-law state that while they may have experienced some problems with their relationship with their mother-in-law, they were eventually able to resolve them with little or no impact on their marriage. Those studies did not consider the effect of the children's relationships with their own parents on their marriages. The purpose of this chapter is to examine adult children's perceptions of how their relationship with their own parents and their spouse's relationship with their parents have impacted their marriage.

SONS' PERCEPTIONS

Nearly all of the sons believed that their relationship with their parents had impacted their marriage. However, for many of them, the effect was an indirect one through their wife. Both Samuel and Ed believed that their relationships

111

with their mothers had a positive effect on their marriages. Samuel stated, "I loved my mother very much. I am able to love my wife so much because of that. I learned to love from my mother. If I had not had such a good mother, though, I don't think I would know how to love [my wife]. You learn how not to be selfish . . . how to think how the other person might feel." However, Samuel did not believe that his wife's poor relationship with her mother and brother had impacted their marriage. He said that, if anything, his wife's troubled relationship with her family made him love her that much more. He explained,

> I do more for my wife because I am all that she has. Her mother and brother just hurt her over and over again. So my family is her family. . . . I wouldn't do anything to hurt her because I know of how much she has been hurt. I always make the holidays nice for her because her mother never did. Plus, I have to make sure that I am around for her because I can't depend on them to look out for her.

Ed also felt that his relationship with his parents had made him a better husband. He explained,

> I learned from my mother and father that it is up to the husband to take care of his wife. . . . I think I am a better husband for doing that. She doesn't have to work unless she wants to, like my mother. She doesn't want for anything. . . . My father was abusive, though, but I have never hit my wife. I saw what it did to my mother . . . and to their marriage. I am hard on my boys, but I teach them that you never hit women.

Thus, while Samuel believed that his relationship with his mother made him a better spouse by making him a more loving person, Ed believed that he was a better spouse by using his parents' marriage as a model of what was good and bad behavior for a husband, replicating what was good, and avoiding what was negative.

The other sons believed that either their relationship with their own parents or their spouse's relationship with her own parents had negatively affected their marriage. Christopher believed that his mother's expectations of him and desire to see him and his children often had caused arguments with his wife throughout their twenty-year marriage, but he did not believe that it had caused any irreparable damage. He explained,

> Well, in fairness to my wife, my mother does want us to be there for every holiday, but I figure that is how mothers are. They want to see their kids and grandkids. I try to make it up to my wife, to do things that she wants to do too. I don't want to make either one of them unhappy. . . . I figure

that I can always make things up to my wife. . . . I want to be a good son as well as a good husband and father. . . . It is not just the holidays, though. My wife also gets upset with my mother for having favorites [among the grandchildren]. I have had to tell her that she can't just do for one and not the others. My wife and I fought a lot about that. My mother also wanted my wife to clean the house better and dress the kids better . . . and take them to voice lessons. I had to tell her that it wasn't worth fighting about with my wife . . . and it wasn't. I just did not like getting between them like that. Otherwise, though, they get along fine. It just created some problems between my wife and me.

When asked how he handled the tension with his wife, Christopher stated, "It helps that my wife shares my views on being respectful of parents. She understands that I want to be a good son and that I want to make my mother happy. She does not do as much for my mother, which is okay. I guess that is our compromise. I don't ask her to do for them."

Christopher also noted that the impact of his relationship with his mother was greater when he and his wife were first married. He explained,

My mother was used to me helping out with my brothers and sisters. So when I got married, she still expected that I would do that and that my wife would do it too. My wife did not like me having to help them so much or [her] having to babysit [them], especially after we had our own baby. The kids would wake up the baby while she was sleeping. . . . Plus, my wife didn't really think that she could make them mind her. . . . Then there were problems when my mother would spank our daughter. We just eventually stopped asking her to babysit because it wasn't worth the fights. . . . No, I don't think it created any long-lasting damage. Maybe my wife isn't as close to my mother as she would be otherwise, but I don't think it really hurt my marriage.

In contrast, Don said that his relationship with his mother severely impacted his marriage during the early years of marriage. He explained,

God, I hate to think about it. It was terrible. One time I just sat in the kitchen and cried. I just couldn't take the tension anymore. My mother just didn't get it . . . or didn't want to get it . . . that I needed more space from her to have [my marriage] . . . that things weren't going to be like they had always been. She just wouldn't make the change. It was a no-brainer that I would pick my wife over my mother . . . but I can see now the stress that it was causing. My mother wanted to be as dependent on me as she had always been, but it really bothered my wife. I felt that I could do both, but my wife did not want me to do both. My father was no help. They had had a very negative divorce.

When asked how it affected his marriage, Don shared the following:

> Well, I would have to say that in the beginning we almost did not get married. The fights were just terrible, especially about the wedding. I found out later that people were actually taking bets about whether my mother would say something when the minister asked [if anyone had reason why we shouldn't marry]. Actually, I thought it was my wife who might call it off, right up to the end. . . . I tried to protect her from some of the things that my mother said. . . . There was a lot that she didn't know. I intercepted all of the e-mails and phone calls. . . . She got along fine with my father and stepmother, though. . . . I think the effects now are minimal, though. We see my mother and I talk to her on the phone, but I have learned to draw boundaries with her. I owe that to my wife.

Tim also felt that his relationship with his mother had affected his marriage, especially while he was engaged and while he was first married. He said,

> The problem is that my mother is divorced. She needs a lot of help around the house, and it bothers my wife that she asks me. What am I supposed to do though? I try to show my mother how to do some things. In defense of my mother, though, there are some things that she really can't do herself. I am the only son. I remind my wife that it won't last forever, and that it could be a lot worse. . . . There was also the problem about holidays. My mother wanted us to spend more holidays with her, but I think that we worked that out.

Later, Tim confided that there had also been some issues with his father that caused problems between him and his wife. He shared the following:

> Well, my father is a little careless. He swears and probably drinks more in front of the kids than he should. My wife doesn't like it, but we have managed to keep that from happening too much now. We don't let my son drive with my father anymore. I did have to agree to that since he drives while he has been drinking. It means that [my son] can't spend the night anymore. I just tell my father that he has to get up early for soccer practice now. It never created the kind of problems that my wife had with my mother, though. We broke up a couple of times because of that. My sister-in-law helped me to understand how my wife was feeling, though.

Thus, several of the sons believed that their mother's dependence on them had resulted in arguments with their wife. Knowing that their mother wanted to spend more time with them also made them feel "caught" between their wife and mother. Only one of the sons mentioned that he believed that there was some jealousy between his wife and mother that caused problems in his marriage. He explained,

> I think that my mother was jealous of my wife. My siblings and I were my mother's whole life. I had never had many girlfriends. I don't know about this kind of thing, but my wife says that my mother looks annoyed whenever I give my wife a kiss or she sits on my lap. I do know that my mother always calls me away when I try to sit with my wife at [my mother's] house. My father doesn't do that, though. My mother has no use for romantic love. . . . My wife? I don't know if she is jealous or not. Maybe. She has no reason to be jealous though. . . . I know that I used to feel torn between them.

WIVES' PERCEPTIONS

A smaller proportion of daughters than sons believed that their relationship with their parents had impacted their marriage. Gail's example was probably the most extreme instance of the effect of the parent-child relationship on marriage. She explained,

> My husband, ex-husband, never liked the fact that I was so close to my mother . . . and my sisters. I was at my mother's house all of the time. But that was how I was raised. Your mother's house is home. Plus, we were young. I just didn't know any better. . . . I was at my mother's most every night. My husband really resented it. I thought that he would get used to it, like my sisters' husbands, but he didn't. . . . My mother used to bad-mouth [my husband]. She never thought he was good enough for my son and me. I shouldn't have listened to her, but I did. So I didn't try to fight it when he wanted to get a divorce. I listened to my mother and took her advice. . . . Now I wonder if it was the right thing to do. I see my ex-husband playing with my son; you can tell that he is his whole life. I could be part of that too if I had listened to my husband instead of to my mother.

Gail's relationship with her mother, then, affected her marriage both because her mother required too much of Gail's time and because she denigrated her husband to Gail. Gail believed that she might not have done the same thing had she married later in life. She explained,

> Now that I am married again, I don't let my mother interfere as much. I still go to visit, but not as much. I have two kids now in sports. . . . Now, though, the problem is my husband's mother. I try not to let her get to me. I don't want to get another divorce. My husband is at her beck-and-call. I

don't go with him, though. I don't really feel welcome. At least my mother
has always welcomed [the sons-in-law].

Other daughters agreed that their mother's need to be close hurt their
marriage. Vicki believed that her mother's insistence that her husband spend
more time with their family was a significant part of their breakup. At the end
of the interview, she added,

> I don't know what I am going to do next time . . . next time that I get
> married or get into a serious relationship. I am afraid to actually . . . to
> ever get involved again. My mother is even more domineering of me since
> I got divorced . . . always wanting to know where I am, always wanting to
> pay for everything, belittling my career. I guess that I will just have to wait
> until my parents are gone [to get married again].

Jennifer stated that her mother's need to be close to her could have affected her marriage, but that her husband stood by her when she needed him.
She explained,

> My family was in a shambles after my father died. My mother was a wreck
> and really needed me. I was dealing with my own family. I just couldn't
> take all of the neediness of my mother. I really was in a bad way. Many
> men would have left someone [like] that. I was screaming and hurting
> myself. I started seeing a therapist and that helped. . . . Now my husband
> gets mad at me if I am short with my mother. My grandparents used to
> visit my mother every single day. It has taken my mother a long time to
> accept that I am not going to be like that . . . that I am not going to tell
> her where I am every minute. It just took her a long time to cut the apron
> strings, and sometimes I have to get after her again. My husband thinks
> that I am unduly harsh, though, and he gets mad at me. He tells me that
> it makes him uncomfortable, so I back off.

Sophie explained that her mother's behavior had nearly cost her her
marriage. The problem with Sophie's mother was not that she wanted to be
too close to Sophie as much as her personality affronted her new son-in-law.
Sophie stated,

> My husband called off the wedding after the rehearsal dinner. He was just
> so appalled by my mother's behavior. She can be very rude, abrasive if you
> don't know her. And she has a tendency to talk about the cost of things.
> . . . So that particular night, she offended [my husband's] uncle. My
> husband was just so embarrassed. I think that the very idea of having her
> around for good terrorized him. . . . Fortunately, it was several days before
> the wedding, and I think that he was able to put it into perspective . . .
> that I am not my mother.

When asked whether or not there was any effect from her relationships with parents on her marriage now, Sophie explained,

Well, my family, . . . it is kind of a tribe mentality. They are all a little crazy. He talks to them nicely on the phone, he is always polite, but he doesn't want to see them any more than he has to. That creates some problems for us, . . . we fight about it . . . because they are my family. I want to see them even though they drive me nuts. We fight to make sure that we are spending equal time with our families. We are both protective of them. It is not like it has caused us to consider divorce or anything, but it does result in fights.

Likewise, Judy's parents' prejudice toward her new husband was affecting her relationship with him. Judy explained, "We need to move because it is so awkward. My mother doesn't want my husband in her house, but we live right upstairs. . . . He doesn't even know whether to say 'hi' when he sees her. . . . It is not good for us. She would like to get my kids on her side too, but they are not as prejudiced, not like her anyway."

Other daughters who had a close relationship with their parents did not believe that the closeness bothered their husband in any way. A few, however, thought that perhaps their *husband's* closeness to their mother had improved their marriage, if only indirectly. For example, Kimberly explained,

It helps . . . that my husband and my mother (plus my father when he was alive) are close. I don't ever have to choose between them. He doesn't mind how much I go to my mother's [house] alone . . . how close we are. [Laughing] In fact, he says that we are two peas in a pod. Maybe if he didn't get along with my mother . . . it might have affected my marriage. It is really hard to imagine, though.

Another daughter said,

I hadn't really thought about it before . . . but my relationship with my mother had probably improved my marriage. She knows how I am, and she will tell me if I am being too critical or too fussy. She will say it, whereas a girlfriend might not. She'll say, "Maybe you are just overtired. You know how you can get." It reminds me that maybe I just have PMS and should just chill out . . . maybe just apologize to my husband before it is too late. She is also close to my husband, so she can smooth his feathers when need be as well.

SUMMARY AND IMPLICATIONS

The likelihood of a couple that is married for the first time divorcing over their lifetime is approximately 43 to 45 percent today.[3] This is down from the peak divorce rate in 1981 of 50 percent of couples eventually divorcing. Still, couples today divorce at rates higher than in many other industrialized countries. Results of this research suggest that adult children's relationships with their parents impact marriage to the point of divorce in only rare cases. It is much more likely that intergenerational relationships result in arguments between the couple or problems early on in the relationship that the couple is able to work out. It is worth noting, however, that this research does not include people who never marry because of problems with their parents, and thus it may underestimate the impact of intergenerational ties on romantic bonds.

The most common effect occurred when close ties between a mother and son resulted in a strained marital relationship. Daughters-in-law became resentful of their mother-in-law's dependence on their husband, which resulted in arguments between husband and wife. Interestingly, though, it was the wife's reaction to her mother-in-law that affected the marriage. Two of the husbands believed that their relationship with their mother actually improved their marriage by making them a more loving husband.

A few close relationships between daughter and mother caused marital rifts, although it was rare. It was much more likely that husbands accepted their wife's close relationship with her parents. This may be due to several factors. We expect daughters to stay close to their parents, while sons are expected to be more independent. Daughters also never spoke of their spouse as being "jealous" of their time with their mother the way that a few of the sons did. This may have to do with the heightened importance of relationality for women or to the fact that mothers of sons continue to depend on their sons more than mothers of daughters, even though mothers and daughters are close. That is, the continued need for the son's time and attention creates a friction between wife and mother-in-law that does not exist for the husband and his mother-in-law. There was no evidence of fathers being dependent on their daughters.

Thus while the instances of harm to marriage are not frequent, they should not be ignored either. Clearly, some marriages are affected by adult children's relationship with their parents. The marriage of an adult child is an important life course event for which not all parents are prepared. Divorced mothers seem particularly prone to depend on their adult sons. Results of this research suggest the need for community support and sometimes counseling at the point when adult children marry. This would help to relieve the tension in relationships between mother-in-law and daughter-in-law as well as improving those marriages that are impacted by parent-child bonds.

Many clergy require some form of premarital counseling before they will perform a marriage ceremony. These sessions could also include discussion of relationships with parents and the need to prioritize the marriage over other relationships after the marriage. Brides- and grooms-to-be who suspect pending problems with their in-laws or problems with their own parents would be well advised to seek counseling to help them and their spouse through the changes that accompany marriage. They may even wish to undergo counseling with their own parents. Parents, too, may need to seek advice, whether from trained professionals, family, or community leaders as they experience changes in their relationships with children following marriage. Like other life course events, a child's marriage creates variation in the parent-child relationship that needs to be accommodated in order for the relationship to be maintained. Family, the community, and helping professionals can play an important role in easing that transition.

· 12 ·

Conclusion

$\mathcal{T}$he genesis of this book is several-fold. In an earlier online discussion of a book on relationships between mothers-in-law and daughters-in-law,[1] readers debated the fairness of sons being expected to "cut the cord" or to separate from their natal family following marriage while daughters remain close to their family.[2] Whether or not there is this expectation and whether or not sons do distance themselves from their natal family following marriage is indeed questionable. This book asks if the old adage "A daughter is a daughter all of her life, but a son is a son 'til he takes him a wife" really is true. This, however, is only part of a greater interest in how parent–adult child relationships change over the life course and, in particular, the impact of marriage on those ties. While the topic of parent–adult child relationships has been a source of great interest over the years, the effect of status transitions on intergenerational relationships has received little attention.[3] The effect of marriage is of particular interest, given all that accompanies it: the introduction of an outsider to the family, the separation and creation of a new nuclear family from each of the natal families, and a redefinition of various family roles. This final chapter attempts to address these overarching questions and what the results tell us about the nature of marriage today.

IS A "SON A SON 'TIL HE TAKES HIM A WIFE"?

Not surprisingly, all but one of the mothers, sons, and daughters that I spoke to had heard of this familiar adage. Over half, though, said that the adage did not apply to their own personal circumstances (a son's relationship with his mother, a mother's relationship with her son, or a daughter's perception of

121

her husband's relationship with his mother), although at least some of these people felt that the adage accurately described other relationships of which they were aware. Fewer of the mothers and daughters than sons believed that the adage accurately described their situation with at least one of their sons or their husband's situation with his mother. Thus, while it is not universal, there is a tendency for some sons to step back from or disengage from their own family following marriage. While it was expected that mothers would be more likely to make this claim, it was actually the sons who were more likely to say that it applied to them.

This difference in expectations for sons versus daughters was exhibited by a difference in actual behavior. That is, couples were more likely to visit the wife's parents than the husband's parents, although the differences were not as large as was expected. Likewise, mothers saw their married daughters more often than their married sons. While earlier researchers have shown that women visit their parents more often than men,[4] this is the first research to ask about the visiting patterns of the couples, which is important in uncovering the process by which men get pulled in to their wife's family. Likewise, women are much more likely to talk to their parents than men are, and they are less likely to call their spouse's family more frequently than their own family in comparison to men. Thus, many people have experienced a family "losing" their son following marriage, which manifests itself in part by married men and women visiting and calling the wife's parents more than the husband's parents. However, it is also much more than that. Even mothers who did not feel that they "lost" their son said that the relationship did change; they described "a lessening of ties" and their sons' "focus being elsewhere." Why do men step back from their natal family when they marry? The answer to this question lies in the above evidence: sons leave their natal family following marriage to the extent that they go over to their wife's side of the family. Why is this the case? Also, why do sons express a need to focus so exclusively on their own nuclear family following marriage while daughters do not?

The reason that many sons tend to "go over to the wife's side of the family," a term used particularly by the mothers following marriage, is based on differing gender expectations of sons versus daughters. It is also the result of women's greater kin-keeping activities within the family and the greater importance they place on relationships. First, many mothers believed that they "lost" their sons due to the sons' tendency to spend more time with their wives' families than their own family. This was due to the expectation that a daughter will stay close to her family after leaving home. In fact, one might argue that a daughter is expected to incorporate her own nuclear family into her natal family. Indeed, all of the mothers, sons, and daughters believed that daughters stayed close to their family following marriage. Thus, daughters, with the help of their own kin, pull their husbands in to their natal families. As the kin keeper of her own family, a daughter sets the social calendar for her and her husband and makes plans for the holidays. Knowing that she is presumed to remain close to her family and often feeling more comfortable with her own family, she plans for the couple to spend more time with her family than his. Because this tendency toward the wife's side of the family is normative, daughters (-in-law) feel justified in the practice, as do many mothers.

Not all of the couples spent more time with her side of the family than his. Many strove for and were cognizant of the need to spend equal amounts of time with both sets of parents. However, it was more often the case that daughters said that they "tried" to spend an equal amount of time with each set of parents and thought that was only fair but the couple still ended up spending more time with the wife's family than the husband's family. Again, this gets back to the normative nature of the arrangement and the highly in-grained expectation that daughters will remain close to their family. It is also consistent with the greater emphasis that women place on personal relation-ships in comparison to men.

Many of the mothers also said that they stayed closer to their daughters in adulthood than their sons because of shared motherhood. However, none of the sons mentioned anything about sharing fatherhood with their father. This, however, may change in the future as the nature of fatherhood requires more involvement with and nurturing of children. For now, the centrality of motherhood for women's identity is an important source of a daughter remaining connected to her own mother.

The final reason that many mothers may "lose" their son following mar-riage is the greater exclusivity in the roles of husband and son versus wife and daughter. The vast majority of the sons in this study stated that they had to lessen their ties with their parents and siblings because of the need to focus on their own [nuclear] family. Some specifically mentioned that this included focusing on their career aspirations. The vast majority of the daughters also had a job or career and were committed to their nuclear family. However, focusing on their own nuclear family was more consistent with being a part of their natal family because of the extent to which their nuclear family was integrated into their extended family. In addition, a large part of their role as mother and wife included being a conduit to the extended family, includ-ing their own parents. Author Nicholas Townsend would argue further that men's work role continues to be a main source of men's identity, perhaps more so than women's identity.[5]

Other researchers have convincingly maintained that the nuclear family is, in fact, "not so nuclear" and is actually embedded in a web of extended family and friends.[6] I would like to argue further that to the extent to which the nuclear family is really part of an extended family, it is foremost a part of the wife's extended family. Indeed, mothers referred to themselves as the "primary grandmother" for their daughters' children but not for their sons' children. Those cases in which the nuclear family was more a part of the husband's extended family usually resulted from an estrangement between the wife and her family, which was rare. There were also cases in which nuclear families moved between both the husband's and the wife's extended families. This often resulted from a very conscientious undertaking on the wife's part (or her husband's part) to include his extended family as much as her extended family. The default, though, was for the nuclear family to be embedded more in the wife's extended family. This is consistent with other findings that the nuclear family is not so nuclear.

Parents, however, do not universally "lose" their sons. The majority of the people interviewed believed that the loss of the son did not occur in their experience. This was somewhat surprising, given the prevalence of adages to the contrary. I argue that a generational shift has resulted in more sons staying close to their family following marriage as a result of changing gender roles within our society. Men and women's roles in the family have become more similar; in particular, men are more involved as fathers. This has had a trickle-down effect resulting in men's greater involvement in the family overall and greater similarity between the roles of son and daughter. No longer are men sitting on the sidelines of family life watching wives and sisters "do it all" and reaping none of the benefits of family life. Likewise, mothers, who now have fewer children and a greater investment in those children, are more likely to take the initiative in keeping their sons as well as their daughters close to them into adulthood. This was evidenced by the many strategies that mothers employed to integrate their daughters-in-law into the family from the very beginning.

Sons were more likely than daughters to say that they had "stepped back from" or "disengaged from" their family of origin. Why would sons be more likely to state this? It may be that sons have internalized the expectations of their gender to become more independent of their family following marriage. Men were as likely as women to have heard the adage, "A daughter is a daughter all of her life, but a son is a son 'til he takes him a wife." However, it may also be that men are just more cognizant than women of the subtle and not-so-subtle ways that they *have* disengaged from their natal family.

Men get pulled in to their wife's family by their wife, their mother-in-law, and sometimes by their children as well. Some of the husbands even said that they felt closer to their wife's family than to their own family.

Many of the mothers intentionally made gestures to integrate their sons-in-law into the family, often when the couple was still dating. Mothers of sons also made attempts to integrate their sons' girlfriends into the family and were often successful in doing so. However, wives were more likely than husbands to further integrate their spouse into the family. Sons would get frustrated when their wife and mother did not get along, but they did not take steps to incorporate their wife into the family. Wives would do things like plan a surprise party for their husband at their *mother's* house where all of the family would be gathered. Wives would also make plans with their parents that included their spouse, or vice versa. The sons, though, were more likely just to stop by their parents' home and to leave any further event planning to their wife. Men also get pulled in to their wife's family through the frequent communication between mother and daughter and through their children. Daughters seemed to rely more on their own mother to assist in caring for the children, which increased men's contact with their spouse's family. Men were more likely to say that their wife's family played a greater role in their children's lives, which increased their contact and sense of being part of the family as well.

IS A "DAUGHTER A DAUGHTER ALL OF HER LIFE"?

All of the respondents stated that the adage "a daughter is a daughter all of her life" applied to their experience as daughters and mothers or their wife's experience as a daughter. Daughters called their parents more often than their in-laws, even when there were problems in the relationship. That is, daughters keep in touch with parents more often than sons, even when they are doing so solely out of obligation. In fact, daughters were more likely to describe "obligatory" relationships with their parents than were sons. Sons who did not feel affection for their parents were more likely to become estranged from their parents. As a result, daughters were less likely to experience "detached" relationships than sons, which included low levels of affection, low contact, and low exchange of resources. Daughters were also less likely to be geographically distant from parents than sons. Those daughters who did live far from parents were more likely to have strained relationships, suggesting that daughters move away from parents when there are problems in the relationship. Women's relative closeness to their parents, particularly their mother, is a result of their socialization while girls and differing gender role expectations within the family.[7] It is also due to the greater emphasis that women place on personal relationships.[8]

HOW MARRIAGE CHANGES RELATIONSHIPS
BETWEEN PARENTS AND ADULT CHILDREN

The second overarching question in this book asks how marriage changes intergenerational relationships. What are the complexities of this transition, and how does it unfold? Many of the mothers said that marriage changed their relationships with their sons, even if only superficially. Nearly half said that their relationship with their son worsened after the son married, but only a couple of mothers said that their relationship with their daughter worsened after her marriage. Mothers of sons were more likely to say that their child's priority and focus were elsewhere and that the relationship now incorporated their child's spouse as well. Mothers of daughters said that they did not have as much time together as they had in the past, especially after grandchildren were born. Overall, there was less change in relationships with daughters after marriage.

The process of change began for some parents and children when the children left home for the first time, for college or for their own apartment. This was true for daughters and for sons, but daughters kept in touch more often, particularly by phoning. Mothers said that they still felt like their children were "theirs," even though they lived away. As one mother said, "His heart still belonged to me. He had his friends at school, but we were still "home." We were where his heart was." Other mothers pointed out that their children were still somewhat dependent on them and that they were still their children's "primary" family then.

Mothers explained that their sons were gone more often when they started dating seriously. Still, girlfriends would sometimes visit along with their sons or sons would be at their parent's home alone. It was not until their sons had their own homes (whether living together with their girlfriend or married) that mothers felt that their focus shifted. Being responsible for their own home, as well as their girlfriend's (or wife's) tendency to spend more time with her family, shifted the son's focus and pulled him in to her family more. A son's living on his own did not make a difference though; it was living with a girlfriend that changed his relationship with his parents. When sons lived alone, they still visited their parents; their parent's home was still their family base. Once they were married or living with a woman, that base shifted to where their wife/girlfriend was. A few of the mothers, however, said that once their sons married, they started spending more, not less, time with their natal family. They suggested that their sons became more family oriented. In fact, a few of the mothers said that their relationships with their sons improved after marriage. This was usually the result of the wife's effort to include her husband's family as well as her own family in their plans.

Daughters had less time for their parents once they left home, whether for college or to work. But other than the amount of time that they had together, mothers felt that the relationships with their daughters did not change after they left home or married. Some of the mothers conscientiously took steps to incorporate their sons-in-law into the family. Interestingly, though, mothers of sons were more likely than mothers of daughters to say that incorporating a child-in-law changed their relationship with their child. It was not until daughters had their own children that mothers became more aware of the need to give their daughters more time with their own families.

A child's divorce also has implications for intergenerational relationships. It has the potential to worsen relationships with daughters if they become more dependent on their parents or if parents worry about them following their divorce. It also worsens relationships with sons, but only if they subsequently move back to their mother's home following their divorce or if the mother blames them for the divorce.

What, then, is it about a relationship with a son that makes this difference? I argue that a relationship with a daughter is so tight and so close that it is not affected by the daughter's marriage. A son's expected independence from his parents, however, affords greater flexibility in terms of closeness. Sons are presumed to pull away. In addition, mothers may feel that their relationship with their son is usurped, to some extent, by his closeness to his wife. Fathers may not feel in competition with sons-in-law to as great an extent because of the daughter's continued closeness to her parents after leaving home and after marriage.

Men thus have a better relationship with their mother before they marry because they have not yet been pulled in to their wife's family, nor have they begun to focus on their own family. In other words, the son's sense of family is still with his parents. Sons become less a part of their natal family after marriage, although some of the mothers said that this change was only a matter of degree. That is, the love was still there, but they did not have as much time together. Others said that it went further than that. They also felt that the love was still there but that their son's heart and focus were with his own family now. I argue that, in contrast to sons, daughters do not leave their own family. Instead, the nuclear family becomes a part of the maternal extended family.

The results of this research show that intergenerational ambivalence is intensified by status transitions. For sons, ambivalence increases as their wife becomes a part of their relationship with their parents and as they begin to focus on their own family. It increases for daughters, but less frequently, when parents are dissatisfied with their daughter's choice of spouse or if they are dissatisfied with the extent to which their son-in-law visits. Not all families experienced an increase in ambivalence. Many of the families had welcomed their child's spouse and eagerly incorporated him or her into the family. This and the parents' attitude toward their child's marriage, more than any other factors, tended to decrease ambivalence for both sons and daughters.

I argue that the importance of status transitions and their effect on intergenerational relationships is little understood in our society. The marriage of a child is a significant event in the family life course, and people tend to pay too little attention to it. Families tend to focus on the wedding and not the marriage. Parents are not prepared for the extent to which their relationships with their children may be affected by their children's marriages and the need to incorporate both sons-in-law and daughters-in-law into the family. Not only does this result in greater ambivalence in the parent-child relationship, but it also results in conflict in the in-law relationship.[9] Families need to be made aware of the changes that may ensue in order to minimize that ambivalence and conflict.

Status transitions have an important effect on intergenerational relationships overall. When one person becomes more or less dependent on the other, brings a new person into the relationship, or otherwise experiences a change in self, the nature of the relationship changes and ties must be renegotiated. Renegotiating family ties upsets the overall equilibrium in the family system. When family members are not prepared for or resistant to the change, conflict can ensue.

Families need to be supported in the same way that we have begun to support couples. The community, church and/or synagogue, and family physicians can do much to encourage families to seek support as they undergo these changes and to be aware that the changes are a natural part of the life course transition and not a personal affront. Family life course educators, where they are available, can also help in this endeavor by making families aware of the significance of the transition. At a minimum, we need to chronicle the changes and their effects and make the information known to families and those who work with them. This book is a part of that endeavor.

Recently, therapists and psychologists have begun using "marriage checkups" as a way of screening for potential marital problems and building strong marriage practices as a response to the noted high divorce rate.[10] Intergenerational relationships are also important to the well-being of adults and to society in general as a source of parental caregiving.[11] Thus, it benefits us all to support those relationships and ease those tensions. The concept of a checkup could be applied to intergenerational relationships at key status transitions, such as at marriage, divorce (the parents' or the child's), or the onset of parental disability or illness. By "checking on" those relationships as they undergo change, providing education, and building communication, practitioners may be able to decrease intergenerational ambivalence and tensions and improve these vital bonds.

Results of this research also point to the need to consider the family context when examining the quality of parent–adult child relationships. Mothers' descriptions of their relationships with their children depended, to a large extent, on both the overall number of children that they had and their availability.[12] Researchers and practitioners need not only to be aware of the differences in the relationships within the family, but also to consider the family structure as one of the determinants of those differences.

THE STATUS OF INTERGENERATIONAL RELATIONSHIPS

The extent of contact between parents and adult children and the importance that adult children place on the relationship, even when spouses and parents do not get along, suggest the resilience of intergenerational relationships and the family at a time in which the family is supposedly falling apart. Alarmists have cited the fractured nature of the family in a postdivorce culture. Whenever possible, they highlight the neglect and abandonment of the elderly. These research results, however, suggest that most intergenerational relationships are strong and robust. In fact, there is some suggestion that intergenerational relationships may be stronger than they have been in the past due to the decrease in family size and the greater investment that parents are placing in their children.

Despite the overall strength of intergenerational relationships, there is a tendency for couples to provide more assistance to the wife's parents than to the husband's parents.[13] In addition, sons take less initiative in maintaining kin relationships.[14] This suggests the potential for unmet need among elders with only sons. It is important for practitioners, in particular, to be aware of this possibility. Elders may not wish to share with others the lack of assistance from their sons and their families. They may also be at higher risk for isolation and depression if they do not have regular contact with adult children and their families. Gerontologists have long noted the need for social support in minimizing the effects of aging.[15]

Results of this research also suggest the need for mothers of sons to embrace their daughters-in-law in the family in order to maintain their relationships with their sons. Many of the mothers in this study experienced little change in their relationships with their sons following marriage. These mothers-in-law were more likely to have incorporated their daughters-in-law into the family and to have consciously created a sense of family through shared interests while their children were growing up. They were also cognizant of and careful not to overstep the boundaries of their sons' marriages. Mothers-in-law who wish to continue to rely on their sons and to enhance their relationships with their married children will find this of interest.

The differences in intergenerational relationships with sons versus daughters may be lessening, however. This is likely the result of men's greater involvement in family life as well as parents raising their sons and daughters more similarly. Younger mothers in this study were less likely to note significant differences in their relationships with their sons versus their daughters, even after marriage.

We must also recognize the variation in intergenerational relationships. While there is certainly diversity within families, there is even greater diversity across families. Just like there is no one "family" format from which others can be judged, there is no one intergenerational relationship that typifies all others. This is important for practitioners, researchers, and theorists to keep in mind while conducting their work. Opportunities still remain to explore that diversity and its causes in greater detail.

MYTH OF THE NUCLEAR FAMILY?

Recent scholars have argued that the nuclear family is not quite as nuclear as we had assumed.[16] Nuclear families are instead part of a well-established and choreographed web of kin and friends on whom they depend for such services as child care. This book shows the extent to which the nuclear family remains a part of the wife's extended family in particular, although some couples maintain extensive contact and involvement with the husband's family as well. I argue that the nuclear family is not so much a myth as just not as independent as we had once assumed. Instead, the nuclear family remains strongly connected to other social institutions, such as the extended family. Those ties remain powerful not only for the exchange of instrumental resources but, as important, for the exchange of affection as well.

Families, however, remain highly committed to the relative importance of the nuclear family and the privacy of marriage. This is best evidenced by the sons' perceived need to focus on their "own" family following marriage and the mothers' reluctant but forceful stance that their sons were right to do so, even if it meant less mother-son interaction. In fact, no one made any statement to suggest that the extended family was more important than the nuclear family. It was expected that daughters would remain close to their parents but that they would still prioritize their own nuclear family. While families today bear little resemblance to the 1950s portrait of the family, the legacy of the nuclear family still continues.

Future research should examine whether and how fathers play a role in this process. This work focused on mothers' perceptions, since they are likely to play the key role in maintaining intergenerational relationships. However, fathers may play an important part in the process of parents' redefining their relationships with adult children and in managing increased distance. Fathers may be negotiating changes in their own relationships with their adult children as well as helping their spouses to manage their relationships. Such a study would shed further light on relationships between fathers and their adult children, an area that has received scant attention in the literature.

THAT GREEDY INSTITUTION CALLED "MARRIAGE"

One of the questions that were first asked in this book is whether the change in intergenerational relationships following marriage suggests that marriage has become a "greedy" institution. That is, does marriage take so much of an adult child's time and emotional resources that it undermines parent–adult child relationships? The results of this research suggest that while relationships do change following marriage, the change is not as great as was originally expected. Also, the change appears to be greater with sons than with daughters, although daughters too spend less time with parents following marriage. This change is beyond an employment effect, since nearly all of the adult children were already working prior to marriage. To some extent, then, marriage is indeed a greedy institution.

What are the cultural characteristics of marriage, then, that make it greedy? Marriages today, referred to as individualized marriages, are expected to provide a source of self-fulfillment and self-realization that earlier companionate marriages did not. However, both are based on the expectation of love within the marriage, which traditional marriage was not. Traditional marriages, which occurred prior to industrialization, were instead based on an alliance between families. As such, the family had a great deal of say and control over the marriage. Today's extended families have relatively little investment in their children's marriages.[17]

With individualistic marriages come high expectations of one's partner. In fact, the movement away from traditional marriages is seen as one of the precipitating factors for the increasing frailty of marriage.[18] Spouses are expected to be best friends and confidants. Couples are expected to share activities and friends and to be available for emotional support. While this has the potential to be a tremendous source of fulfillment, it also has the potential to add to the demands on a spouse.

Marriage appears to have a greater impact on mother-son relationships than on mother-daughter relationships. That is, marriage is greedier toward men than women with respect to intergenerational relationships. Despite the increased importance of work in women's lives, men's masculinity is even more deeply tied to their role as provider as well as their work identity. In contrast, relational ties remain more important to women.[19] Men's relationships with parents will continue to take a back seat to the extent that their roles remain focused on provision for the nuclear family and work.

The nuclear family is also a greedy institution. It emphasizes the needs of only one's immediate family: spouse and children. Aging parents are relegated to the extended family, opening up the possibility for unmet needs in old age. Adult relationships with siblings are also neglected in midlife, while one is focused on one's nuclear family. Research suggests though that sibling relationships become important again in later life.[20]

How will marriage change in the future and what are the likely implications for intergenerational relationship? It is argued that marriage is increasingly becoming available for only those who are able to obtain economic stability.[21] Emotional stability and the luck of choosing a partner who can change with you are also important precursors to marriage. These factors also limit the number of people who can sustain a marriage. Thus, marriage may become only one of a group of living and parenting arrangements for many adults. Both its rewards and its impact may be further circumscribed.

Intergenerational relationships will continue to be challenged by the myriad living arrangements from which adult children choose. Whether adult sons and daughter are in long-term cohabiting relationships with their own children or serial marriages with offspring spread across those marriages, parents and adult children will continue to need to find a common ground on which to maintain their relationships. Likewise, mothers, children, and children-in-law will continue to be obliged to develop new strategies to make those relationships work. For now though, marriage and the nuclear family are here to stay.

Appendix 1: Methodology

$\mathscr{T}$his study is based on interviews with twenty-five mothers who had at least one married son and one married daughter as well as twenty-five adult children (eight men and seventeen women) who had at some point been married for at least two years. Respondents were recruited through newspaper advertisements in both the local purchased newspaper and a free weekly newspaper as well as by fliers placed in a number of areas of the city. Purposive sampling was used to obtain respondents from various income and educational levels as well as various ages and lengths of time married. All male respondents and individuals from poorer areas of the city were included, while some middle-class women (estimated by area of the city they lived in, educational level, and main occupation) were passed over. The data include daughters as young as twenty-eight years of age and mothers as old as eighty-three years of age.

The advertisements stated that the interview pertained to how parent–adult child relationships changed or did not change after the child's marriage. The respondents were also told that they would receive twenty-five dollars for the interview and that the results were confidential. The ad for mothers was placed first, and the ads for adult children were placed several months later. Mothers began calling immediately, and there were more than the targeted twenty-five respondents by the end of the first week. Adult children were harder to recruit; two ads had to be placed in each of the newspapers to locate the minimum twenty-five respondents.

Results are not necessarily representative of the overall population. However, they can be instructive in explaining how relationships change after marriage. Despite the fact that this was not a randomly drawn sample, it does include people from across all educational and income levels (including men and women who were unemployed or receiving disability income as well as those who finished only the ninth grade). The data also include people with a wide variety of intergenerational relationships and experiences. Only two minority respondents were interviewed, but respondents come from a variety of ethnic backgrounds that are representative of the area. See tables A1.1 and A1.2 for the characteristics of the sample.

Respondents were told that they could be interviewed at the university, in their home, or in a coffee shop/restaurant of their choosing. Most of the interviews took place in the respondent's home. A standardized protocol was used for all interviews, with a structured questionnaire and the same interviewer. All respondents were interviewed alone, although occasionally a child would walk through the room. Interviews took anywhere from one and a half to three and a half hours. Periodically respondents had to be called a second time in order to clarify information following the interview.

Twenty-five adult children were interviewed, including seventeen women and eight men. Each of the adult children was asked to describe: (a) how often they and their spouse visit their parents and in-laws together and separately and (b) how often each of them calls their parents and in-laws. As a result, there is data on twenty-five couples, including twenty-five wives and twenty-five husbands. It should be made clear that the twenty-five mothers who were sampled are not the mothers of these adult children, with the exception of two mothers. The three daughters of these two mothers were interviewed after their mothers suggested their services. However, the interviewer was very careful to make sure that the daughters were truly volunteering and understood that their responses were confidential. This situation was generally avoided, however, to maximize the quality of the data. It was expected that mothers and adult children might not be as honest in their answers if they thought that the other was being interviewed. As a result there are actually two subsets of data, one of adult children and one of mothers of adult children. Both subsets of data are used in this analysis. The first and last names of all of the participants and their families have been changed to maintain confidentiality.

Qualitative data allow us to answer the questions presented in the literature. The strength of this particular data set is that it is rich in information on men's and women's perceptions of why they see more of one side of the family than the other, mothers' detailed perceptions of the myriad ways that they try to maintain contact with adult children, and the process by which men get pulled in to their wife's family. In other words, the strength of the qualitative data is that it allows us to answer questions about process, change, and the mechanisms through which family members create the patterns found in quantitative data.

Another strength of this particular data is that it includes information on both mothers and adult children. It is particularly important to talk to both

Table A1.1. Description of the Adult Children

Relationship Status:	N
Sons:	8 (32%)
Daughters:	17 (68%)
N =	25

Age:	N
20–29:	1 (4%)
30–39:	4 (16%)
40–49:	14 (56%)
50–59:	6 (24%)
N =	25

Marital Status:	N
Married:	19 (76%)
Divorced:	5 (20%)
Remarried:	1 (4%)
N =	25

Number of Years Married	N
2–5:	8 (32%)
6–9:	5 (20%)
10–19:	5 (20%)
20 or more:	7 (28%)
N =	25

Educational Level:	N
Some High School:	2 (8%)
High School Graduate:	4 (16%)
Some College:	4 (16%)
College Degree:	9 (36%)
(Including 3 Associate Degrees)	
Master's Degree:	5 (20%)
PhD:	1 (4%)
N =	25

Race:	N
White	23 (92%)
Latino	1 (4%)
African American	1 (4%)
N =	25

Table A1.2.   Description of the Mothers

Age:	N
40–49:	0 (0%)
50–59:	7 (28%)
60–69:	10 (40%)
70–79:	6 (24%)
80+:	2 (8%)
N =	25

Marital Status:	N
Married:	14 (56%)
Widowed:	7 (28%)
Divorced:	3 (12%)
Remarried:	1 (4%)
N =	25

Educational Level:	N
Some High School:	2 (8%)
High School Graduate:	8 (32%)
Some College:	2 (8%)
College Degree:	5 (20%)
Master's Degree:	7 (28%)
JD:	1 (4%)
N =	25

Number of Children:	N
2:	9 (36%)
3:	12 (48%)
4:	4 (16%)
N =	25

generations, given the topic. For example, mothers were much more aware of the changes in the relationship following marriage than were adult children while children were more aware of the timing of events and the intricacies of keeping in contact. A complete picture of the process by which changes unfold following marriage would not be possible without interviewing both mothers and adult children.

DATA ANALYSIS

The researcher transcribed all of the interviews to ensure data quality and maximum knowledge of the data. Content analysis was used. The researcher would record and categorize consistent themes that emerged from the data. This required a minimum of two readings of all of the transcripts, first to look for emerging themes and second to categorize the data. More often, however, three or more readings were required to categorize responses that were not obvious, that is, those that did not fit neatly into any one category.

MEASURES

Extent of Contact

Adult children were asked whether or not the couple sees more of the wife's relatives or the husband's relatives, how often both the husband and wife call their parents and in-laws, and whether each of them calls their own parents more than the spouse's parents. Not all children, nor all parents, were currently married, however. Adult children who were divorced were asked about the level of contact that they and their spouse had with parents while they were married. Adult children whose parents were divorced were asked about separate contact with each parent. Those whose parents or in-laws were deceased were asked about contact on average before the parents' death. If the level of contact had changed because of an illness, contact both before and after the illness was recorded. Both measures were recorded if respondents differentiated contact with their mothers versus their fathers.

"Losing" One's Son or Daughter

Mothers of adult children were also interviewed. They were asked whether or not they felt that they had "lost" their sons or daughters when they married. The interviewer explained that this included the child stepping back from the natal family after marriage, cutting off ties, or otherwise disengaging from the natal family. Mothers were also asked how their relationship with the child changed after marriage, if at all. The mothers sometimes responded that this change was a matter of degree. The researcher then categorized the cases according to the extent of change. Those cases in which the child called less after marriage or visited less but still acted as part of the family were counted as the parent not "losing" the child according to the mother. Only those parents who described disengagement, significant change, or loss were categorized as having "lost" their son or daughter. Mothers were also asked to describe what they did to maintain contact with their adult children after marriage.

Adult children were asked whether or not they felt that they had "stepped back" from their natal families when they married, become less a part of the family, or disengaged from the family. Again, cases were categorized according to the degree and were based on key words used by the respondent.

Appendix 2: Interview Guidelines

INTERVIEW OF MOTHERS

A. Background
 1. Are you currently married, widowed, or divorced?
 2. Is your current spouse the father of your children or are you remarried?
 3. If you have been divorced, how old were your children when you divorced?
 4. If you are remarried, how old were your children when you remarried?
 5. Do you belong to a religious group, and if so, which one?
 6. Do you belong to an ethnic group, and if so, which one?
 7. What is your current age?
 8. What was your highest level of education completed?
B. Family Structure
 1. How many children do you have?
    a. Are any of these children your stepchildren? Which ones?
 2. What are your children's ages?
 3. Are those children married, divorced, or single?
 4. Where does each child live?
 5. How long has each child been married?
 6. How many (of your grand) children does each child have?
C. Quality of Relationship with Children [Ask for each child.]
 1. Please describe your current relationship with Child #1 (Name).
 2. How often do you see him or her?
 3. How often do you talk on the phone or e-mail one another?

4. What is the nature of your visits (long or short, at whose house, for what occasions etc.)?
5. What do you usually talk to this child about?
6. Do you believe that you are emotionally close to this child? If not, how would you describe your relationship?
7. Do you experience conflict with this child? What is it most often about?
8. Do you rely on this child for emotional support or sharing personal information? Could you rely on him or her for assistance?
9. Is there any tension or uncomfortableness in your relationship?
10. If you are divorced or remarried, please describe your child's relationship with his or her father.
11. If your child's relationship is different with his or her father than it is with you, please describe.

D. When Child Married [Ask for each child.]
   1. When Child #1 got married, how did his or her relationship with you change *if at all?*
   2. What about his/her relationship with their father and siblings?
   3. Had he or she lived away before? For how long?
   4. How old was this child when he or she got married?
   5. How did you get along with his or her spouse around the time of marriage?
   6. Did this son or daughter move from the area after they got married?
   7. Did he or she spend less time with the family?
      a. How did this come about?
      b. When did it happen?
      c. Was it gradual or sudden?
   8. Did he or she call less often?
      a. How did this come about?
      b. When did it happen?
      c. Was it gradual or sudden?
   9. Did he or she attend family activities and holidays as often?
      a. How did this come about?
      b. When did it happen?
      c. Was it gradual or sudden?
      d. Was there tension around the holidays?
      e. How do you divide holidays up?
   10. Did he or she act as though they were as much a part of the family as before?
      a. How did this come about?
      b. When did it happen?
      c. Was it gradual or sudden?

11. Did you feel like you "lost" your son or daughter when they married? This would include your child stepping back from the family after he or she married, cutting off ties, or otherwise disengaging from the family.
12. What did you do to maintain contact with your child after he or she married?
13. What was your relationship with your own in-laws like?

E. Maintaining Contact [Ask for each child.]
  1. How often does Child #1 call you?
     a. How often do you call him or her?
  2. How often do you see him or her?
  3. When you get together with Child #1, who usually makes the arrangements?
  4. Do you spend more time with your child alone or with their spouse as well?
  5. What are visits like when his or her spouse is there? How are they different from when your child is alone?
  6. Who initiates the contact with your grandchildren?
  7. How often does your child spend with his or her own in-laws?
     a. Does this child see more of his or her in-laws or you?
     b. To your knowledge, how often does your child call his or her in-laws?

F. Child-in-Law [Ask for each one.]
  1. What is your relationship like with Child #1's husband or wife?
  2. Has it always been like that? How has it changed?
  3. Does this *couple* spend more time with your family or the other in-laws? Why?
  4. Do you think that this child-in-law feels a part of your family? Why or why not?
  5. What did you do to make this child feel a part of your family?
  6. What is this person's relationship like with their own (natal) family?
     a. With their own mother, particularly?
     b. How often does he or she call her own parents?

G. Comparison of Relationships with Children
  1. Which of your children do you feel closest to and why?
  2. Which of your children do you feel *least* connected to and why?
  3. Do you feel a part of each of your children's families? Why or why not?
  4. Which of your children do you think provides you the most emotional support?
  5. Which of your children can you rely on for assistance?

6. Do you think that all of your children remained a part of the family after they married?

H. Attitudes
   1. Have you heard the saying, "A daughter is a daughter all of her life, but a son is a son till he takes him a wife"? Do you think this saying is an accurate depiction of what happens in families when children marry?
   2. Is it an accurate depiction of your family?
   3. Did you expect your son to be more independent of your family when he grew up than your daughter?
   4. Did you expect your daughter to remain closer to your family when she grew up than your son?
   5. What about your husband? What do you think were his expectations?
   6. What did you expect would happen when each of your children married?
      a. Did you expect them to stay as involved in the family as before?
      b. Did you expect them to concentrate more on their own family?
      c. Did you expect them to be more involved in their spouse's family?
   7. Do you think it is "fair" or "reasonable" for couples to spend more time with the wife's family than with the husband's family?
   8. How do you think you conveyed your feelings (on this subject) to your children?

I. Miscellanea
   1. How did you and your husband divide your time when you first got married?
   2. Please identify the category that comes closest to your annual family income (*provide card*).

INTERVIEW WITH ADULT CHILDREN

A. Background
   1. How many years have you been married?
   2. Is this your first marriage or second marriage?
      a. How long were you previously married?
      b. At what age were you married?
   3. Do you belong to a religious group, and if so, which one?
   4. Do you belong to an ethnic group, and if so, which one?
   5. What is your current age?
   6. What was your highest level of education completed?

B. Degree of Contact with Natal Family [If this varies by parent, ask for each.]
   1. How often do you *see* your parents?
     a. Is this usually with your spouse or alone?
   2. How often do you see your siblings?
   3. How often do you *call* your parents?
     a. Does your spouse usually speak to your parents too?
   4. Who usually initiates calls and visits, you or your parents?
   5. What is the nature of visits like with your parents?
     a. How long are they?
     b. Where do they usually take place?
     c. Is there usually an occasion?
   6. Do you attend family get-togethers and holidays with each parent? How do you divide holidays?
   7. Do you make sure that your children see your parents or does someone else usually oversee that? If so, who?

C. Quality of Relationship with Parents [Note: Ask for each parent if the parents are divorced or if the respondent describes different relationships with parents above.]
   1. How would you describe your relationship with your parents?
   2. How would you describe your relationship with your siblings?
   3. Do you feel emotionally close to your parents?
   4. Is there conflict in the relationship?
   5. What about tension or feeling uncomfortable?
   6. Do you and your parents provide one another with emotional support?
   7. Would you provide one another with assistance if needed (such as financial assistance, help with moving etc.)?
   8. What is your spouse's relationship like with your parents?

D. Comparison with In-laws
   1. Who do you see more often, your parents or your in-laws?
   2. With whom do you talk on the phone more often, your parents or your in-laws?
   3. What about your spouse?
     a. Who does he/she see more?
     b. Who does he/she call more?
   4. Would you say that you feel closer to your parents or to your in-laws?
   5. Which set of parents do you spend more time with as a couple?

E. Childhood Expectations
   1. While you were growing up, were you encouraged to become independent from your family when you became an adult?
   2. Were you encouraged to remain close to your family when you grew up?

3. Were you expected to put your spouse and children before your parents and siblings when you got married?
4. Did your parents expect you to remain a part of their family as well once you married? To what extent?
5. Have you heard the saying, "A daughter is a daughter all of her life, but a son is a son till he gets him a wife"?
   a. Do you think that is true of your own example? What about your spouse?
   b. Who or where did you get that expectation from?

F. Marriage
   1. When you were first married, did you and your spouse spend more time with your family or his/her family? Why?
   2. Had you ever lived away before you got married? For how long?
   3. Did you spend less time with your parents than you had before you got married?
      a. How did this come about?
      b. When did it happen?
      c. Was it gradual or sudden?
   4. Did you talk on the phone less?
      a. How did this come about?
      b. When did it happen?
      c. Was it gradual or sudden?
   5. Did you go to fewer family activities?
      a. How did this come about?
      b. When did it happen?
      c. Was it gradual or sudden?
   6. Who initiated getting together with your parents?
   7. Did you usually get together with your parents alone or with your spouse?
   8. Did you feel less a part of the family?
   9. *Whom* did you think of as your family at that time?
   10. Do you feel that you stepped back from your family when you got married, became less a part of the family, or disengaged from the family?
   11. What about for your spouse and his or her family? Please explain.

G. Attitudes
   1. Do you think you are as close to your family as before you got married?
   2. Do you feel as though you are as much a part of the family as before you got married?

3. Do you feel as though you have one, two, or three families? Please explain.
4. Do you support the saying, "A daughter is a daughter all of her life, but a son is a son till he gets him a wife"? That is, do you apply it to your own situation?
5. Would your spouse mind if you wanted the two of you to spend more time with your family?
   a. What about seeing more of your family alone?
   b. Would he mind the two of you seeing more of his own family?
6. Do you think it is "fair" or "reasonable" for women to want to spend more time with their own families than their husbands' families?
7. Do you think there is a double standard in our society that women can remain close to their parents when they get married but men are expected to cut the ties?
8. Did this happen in your case?
9. Did your spouse want you to spend less time with your parents and family once you were married?
10. Did you want to spend less time with your family?
11. Why then do you spend less time with your family?
12. Who would you define as *your* family?
13. Do you think that you are as much a part of your family as before you got married? Why or why not?

H. Miscellanea

Please indicate the category that comes closest to your annual family income (*provide card*).

Notes

1. INTRODUCTION

1. Deborah M. Merrill, *Mothers-in-Law and Daughters-in-Law: Understanding the Relationship and What Makes Them Friends or Foe* (Westport, CT: Praeger Publishers, 1997).

2. *Salon*, http://letters.salon.com/mwt/broadsheet/2007/10/17/mother_in_law/view/index1.html?sh (retrieved 10/18/2007 and 10/19/2007).

3. Vern Bengtson, Timothy Biblarz, and Robert Roberts, *How Families Still Matter: A Longitudinal Study of Youth in Two Generations* (New York: Cambridge University Press, 2002); John R. Logan and Glenna D. Spitze, *Family Ties: Enduring Relations between Parents and Their Grown Children* (Philadelphia, PA: Temple University Press, 1996); Diane Lye, "Adult Child-Parent Relationships," *Annual Review of Sociology* 22 (1996): 79–102; Merril Silverstein and Vern Bengtson, "Intergenerational Solidarity and the Structure of Adult Child-Parent Relationships in American Families," *American Journal of Sociology* 103 (1997): 429–60; Debra Umberson, "Relationships between Adult Children and Their Parents: Psychological Consequences for Both Generations," *Journal of Marriage and Family* 54 (1992): 664–74.

4. Karl Pillemer and J. Jill Suitor, "Exploring Mothers' Ambivalence toward Their Adult Children," *Journal of Marriage and Family* 64 (2002): 602–13.

5. William S. Aquilino, "Two Views of One Relationship: Comparing Parents' and Young Adult Children's Reports on the Quality of Intergenerational Relationships," *Journal of Marriage and Family* 61 (1999): 858–70.

6. Karen L. Fingerman, *Aging Mothers and Their Adult Daughters: A Study in Mixed Emotions* (New York: Springer, 2001); Karen L. Fingerman, *Mothers and Their Adult Daughters* (Amherst, NY: Prometheus Books, 2003); Gunhild O. Hagestad, "The Family: Women and Grandparents as Kinkeepers," in *Our Aging Society* (New York: Norton, 1986), 141–60; Glenna Spitze and John Logan, "More

147

Evidence on Women (and Men) in the Middle," *Research on Aging* 12 (1990): 182–98.

7. Gayle Kaufman and Peter Uhlenberg, "Effects of Life Course Transitions on the Quality of Relationships between Adult Children and Their Parents," *Journal of Marriage and Family* 60 (1998): 924–38.

8. Eunju Lee, Glenna Spitze, and John R. Logan, "Social Support to Parents-in-Law: The Interplay of Gender and Kin Hierarchies," *Journal of Marriage and Family* 65 (2003): 396–403.

9. Kim Shuey and Melissa Hardy, "Assistance to Aging Parents and Parents-in-Law: Does Lineage Affect Family Allocation Decisions?" *Journal of Marriage and Family* 65 (2003): 418–31.

10. Lee, Spitze, and Logan, "Social Support to Parents-in-Law: The Interplay of Gender and Kin Hierarchies."

11. Lewis Coser and Rose Coser, *Greedy Institutions: Patterns of Undivided Commitment* (New York: Free Press, 1974).

12. Natalia Sarkisian and Naomi Gerstel, "Till Marriage Do Us Part: Adult Children's Relationships with Their Parents," *Journal of Marriage and Family* 70 (2008): 360–76.

13. Stephanie Coontz, *Marriage, a History: How Love Conquered Marriage* (New York: Penguin, 2005).

14. Paul Amato, "Tension between Institutional and Individual Views of Marriage," *Journal of Marriage and Family* 66 (2004): 959–65; Paul R. Amato, Alan Booth, David R. Johnson, and Stacy J. Rogers, *Alone Together: How Marriage in America Is Changing* (Cambridge, MA: Harvard University Press, 2007); Andrew Cherlin, "The Deinstitutionalization of American Marriage," *Journal of Marriage and Family* 66 (2004): 848–61; Andrew Cherlin, *The Marriage-Go-Round: The State of Marriage and the Family in America Today* (New York: Alfred A. Knopf, 2009); Linda Waite and Maggie Gallagher, *The Case for Marriage: Why Married People are Happier, Healthier, and Better Off Financially* (New York: Doubleday, 2000).

15. Kathryn Edin and Maria Kefalas, *Promises I Can Keep* (Berkeley: University of California Press, 2005).

16. Alice Rossi and Peter Rossi, *Of Human Bonding: Parent-Child Relations across the Life Course* (New York: Aldine de Gruyter, 1990); Arland Thornton, Terri L. Orbuch, and William G. Axinn, "Parent-Child Relations during the Transition to Adulthood," *Journal of Family Issues* 16 (1995): 538–64.

17. Vern Bengtson, Carolyn Rosenthal, and Linda Burton, "Families and Aging: Diversity and Heterogeneity," in *Handbook of Aging and the Social Sciences* (San Diego, CA: Academic Press, 1990), 263–87; John R. Logan and Glenna D. Spitze, *Family Ties: Enduring Relations between Parents and Their Grown Children* (Philadelphia, PA: Temple University Press, 1996); Diane Lye, "Adult Child-Parent Relationships," *Annual Review of Sociology* 22 (1996): 79–102; Phyllis Moen, "Gender, Age, and the Life Course," in *Handbook of Aging and the Social Sciences* (San Diego, CA: Academic Press, 1996), 171–87; Alice Rossi, "Intergenerational Relations: Gender, Norms, and

Behavior," in *Changing Contracts across Generations* (New York: Aldine de Gruyter, 1994), 191–211; Merril Silverstein and Vern Bengtson, "Intergenerational Solidarity and the Structure of Adult Child-Parent Relationships in American Families," *American Journal of Sociology* 103 (1997): 429–60.

18. Russell A. Ward, Glenna Spitze, and Glenn Deane, "The More the Merrier? Multiple Parent-Adult Child Relations," *Journal of Marriage and Family* 71 (2009): 161–73.

19. See appendix 1 for a discussion of the methodology.

2. ILLUSTRATIONS OF INTERGENERATIONAL RELATIONSHIPS

1. This chapter highlights two families in which both the mother and child were interviewed in order to provide the most comprehensive view of the relationships as possible.

3. RELATIONSHIPS BETWEEN PARENTS AND ADULT CHILDREN

1. Vern Bengtson, Timothy Biblarz, and Robert Roberts, *How Families Still Matter: A Longitudinal Study of Youth in Two Generations* (New York: Cambridge University Press, 2002); John R. Logan and Glenna D. Spitze, *Family Ties: Enduring Relations between Parents and Their Grown Children* (Philadelphia, PA: Temple University Press, 1996); Diane Lye, "Adult Child–Parent Relationships," *Annual Review of Sociology* 22 (1996): 79–102; Merril Silverstein and Vern Bengtson, "Intergenerational Solidarity and the Structure of Adult Child–Parent Relationships in American Families," *American Journal of Sociology* 103 (1997): 429–60; Debra Umberson, "Relationships between Adult Children and Their Parents: Psychological Consequences for Both Generations," *Journal of Marriage and Family* 54 (1992): 664–74.

2. Ge Lin and Peter Rogerson, "Elderly Parents and the Geographic Availability of Their Adult Children," *Research on Aging* 17, no. 3 (1995): 303–31.

3. Ingrid A. Connidis, *Family Ties and Aging* (Thousand Oaks, CA: Sage Publications, 2001); Silverstein and Bengtson, "Intergenerational Solidarity."

4. William S. Aquilino, "Two Views of One Relationship: Comparing Parents' and Young Adult Children's Reports on the Quality of Intergenerational Relationships," *Journal of Marriage and Family* 61 (1999): 858–70.

5. Karen L. Fingerman, Elizabeth Hay, and Kira S. Birditt, "The Best of Ties, the Worst of Ties: Close, Problematic, and Ambivalent Social Relationships," *Journal of Marriage and Family* 66 (2004): 792–808.

6. Karl Pillemer and J. Jill Suitor, "Exploring Mothers' Ambivalence toward Their Adult Children," *Journal of Marriage and Family* 64 (2002): 602–13.

7. Russell A. Ward, Glenna Spitze, and Glenn Deane, "The More the Merrier? Multiple Parent–Adult Child Relations," *Journal of Marriage and Family* 71 (2009): 161–73.

8. Pillemer and Suitor, "Exploring Mothers' Ambivalence."

9. Alice Rossi and Peter Rossi, *Of Human Bonding: Parent-Child Relations across the Life Course* (New York: Aldine de Gruyter, 1990).

10. Marilyn Coleman, Larry H. Ganong, and Tanya C. Rothrauff, "Racial and Ethnic Similarities and Differences in Beliefs about Intergenerational Assistance to Older Adults after Divorce and Remarriage," *Family Relations* 55 (2006): 165–76.

11. Lye, "Adult Child–Parent Relationships."

12. Ann Goetting, "Patterns of Support among In-Laws in the United States," *Journal of Family Issues* 11, no. 1 (1990): 67–90; Eunju Lee, Glenna Spitze, and John R. Logan, "Social Support to Parents-in-Law: The Interplay of Gender and Kin Hierarchies," *Journal of Marriage and Family* 65 (2003): 396–403; Kim Shuey and Melissa Hardy, "Assistance to Aging Parents and Parents-in-Law: Does Lineage Affect Family Allocation Decisions?" *Journal of Marriage and Family* 65 (2003): 418–31.

13. Rossi and Rossi, *Of Human Bonding*.

14. Andrea E. Willson, Kim M. Shuey, and Glenn H. Elder Jr., "Ambivalence in the Relationships of Adult Children to Aging Parents and In-Laws," *Journal of Marriage and Family* 65 (2003): 1055–72.

15. Lye, "Adult Child–Parent Relationships."

16. Joan Aldous, "New Views of Grandparents in Intergenerational Context," *Journal of Family Issues* 16 (1995): 104–22.

17. Jacob Climo, *Distant Parents* (New Brunswick, NJ: Rutgers University Press, 1992).

18. Gayle Kaufman and Peter Uhlenberg, "Effects of Life Course Transitions on the Quality of Relationships between Adult Children and Their Parents," *Journal of Marriage and Family* 60 (1998): 924–38.

19. Deborah M. Merrill, *Mothers-in-Law and Daughters-in-Law: Understanding the Relationship and What Makes Them Friends or Foe* (Westport, CT: Praeger Publishers, 2007).

20. This typology is based on that developed by Ingrid Connidis, *Family Ties and Aging*, 126.

21. Goetting, "Patterns of Support among In-Laws"; Lee, Spitze, and Logan, "Social Support to Parents-in-Law"; Shuey and Hardy, "Assistance to Aging Parents and Parents-in-Law."

22. Connidis, *Family Ties and Aging*.

23. Goetting, "Patterns of Support among In-Laws"; Lee, Spitze, and Logan, "Social Support to Parents-in-Law"; Shuey and Hardy, "Assistance to Aging Parents and Parents-in-Law."

24. Kaufman and Uhlenberg, "Effects of Life Course Transitions."

4. GENDER DIFFERENCES IN CONTACT WITH PARENTS AND IN-LAWS: DO COUPLES SEE MORE OF HER FAMILY THAN HIS?

1. Alan Booth and Paul R. Amato, "Parental Marital Quality, Parental Divorce, and Relations with Parents," *Journal of Marriage and Family* 56 (1994): 21–34; Alice Rossi and Peter Rossi, *Of Human Bonding: Parent-Child Relations across the Life Course* (New York: Aldine de Gruyter, 1990); Gunhild O. Hagestad, "The Family: Women and Grandparents as Kinkeepers," in *Our Aging Society* (New York: Norton, 1986), 141–60.

2. Karen L. Fingerman, *Aging Mothers and Their Adult Daughters: A Study in Mixed Emotions* (New York: Springer, 2001); Karen L. Fingerman, *Mothers and Their Adult Daughters* (Amherst, NY: Prometheus Books, 2003); Hagestad, "The Family"; Glenna Spitze and John Logan, "More Evidence on Women (and Men) in the Middle," *Research on Aging* 12 (1990a): 182–98; Russell A. Ward, Glenna Spitze, and Glenn Deane, "The More the Merrier? Multiple Parent-Adult Child Relations," *Journal of Marriage and Family* 71 (2009): 161–73.

3. Leora Lawton, Merril Silverstein, and Vern L. Bengtson, "Solidarity between Generations in Families," in *Intergenerational Linkages: Hidden Connections in American Society* (New York: Springer Publishers, 1994), 19–42; Rossi and Rossi, *Of Human Bonding*; Spitze and Logan, "More Evidence"; Glenna Spitze and John Logan, "Sons, Daughters, and Intergenerational Social Support," *Journal of Marriage and Family* 52 (1990): 420–30; Debra Umberson, "Relationships between Adult Children and their Parents: Psychological Consequences for Both Generations," *Journal of Marriage and Family* 54 (1992): 664–74.

4. Glenna Spitze, John Logan, Glenn Deane, and Suzanne Zerger, "Adult Children's Divorce and Intergenerational Relationships," *Journal of Marriage and Family* 56 (1994): 279–93.

5. Spitze and Logan, "Sons, Daughters, and Intergenerational Social Support."

6. Eunju Lee, Glenna Spitze, and John Logan, "Social Support to Parents-in-Law: The Interplay of Gender and Kin Hierarchies," *Journal of Marriage and Family* 65 (2003): 396–403.

7. Kim Shuey and Melissa Hardy, "Assistance to Aging Parents and Parents-in-Law: Does Lineage Affect Family Allocation Decisions?" *Journal of Marriage and Family* 65 (2003): 418–31.

8. Shuey and Hardy, "Assistance to Aging Parents and Parents-in-Law."

9. Marilyn Coleman, Larry Ganong, and Susan M. Cable, "Beliefs about Women's Intergenerational Family Obligations to Provide Support before and after Divorce and Remarriage," *Journal of Marriage and Family* 56 (1997): 165–76; Rossi and Rossi, *Of Human Bonding*.

10. Rossi and Rossi, *Of Human Bonding*.

11. Andrea E. Willson, Kim M. Shuey, and Glenn H. Elder Jr., "Ambivalence in the Relationships of Adult Children to Aging Parents and In-Laws," *Journal of Marriage and Family* 65 (2003): 1055–72.

12. Rossi and Rossi, *Of Human Bonding*.

13. Lee, Spitze, and Logan, "Social Support to Parents-in-Law."

14. Lee, Spitze, and Logan, "Social Support to Parents-in-Law.

15. These comparisons were made only for mothers who had at least one son and daughter living at a similar distance.

16. Deb's mother was currently in a nursing home with dementia.

17. Carol Gilligan, *In a Different Voice: Psychological Theory and Women's Development* (Cambridge, MA: Harvard University Press, 1982); Judith V. Jordan, *Relational-Cultural Therapy* (Washington, DC: American Psychological Association, 2009); Jean Baker Miller, *Toward a Psychology of Women* (Boston, MA: Beacon Press, 1986); Cristina Robb, *This Changes Everything: The Relational Revolution in Psychology* (New York: Picador, 2007).

18. John R. Logan and Glenna D. Spitze, *Family Ties: Enduring Relations between Parents and their Grown Children* (Philadelphia, PA: Temple University Press, 1996); Claude Fischer, *America Calling: A Social History of the Telephone to 1940* (Berkeley: University of California Press, 1992).

19. Fischer, *America Calling*.

20. Lee, Spitze, and Logan, "Social Support to Parents-in-Law."

21. The mothers were less likely to call their sons multiple times a day. Only one son called his mother multiple times during the day.

22. Lee, Spitze, and Logan, "Social Support to Parents-in-Law."

23. Lee, Spitze, and Logan, "Social Support to Parents-in-Law.

24. Deborah M. Merrill, *Mothers-in-Law and Daughters-in-Law: Understanding the Relationship and What Makes Them Friends or Foe* (Westport, CT: Praeger Publishers, 2007).

5. "A DAUGHTER IS A DAUGHTER ALL OF HER LIFE, BUT A SON IS A SON 'TIL HE TAKES HIM A WIFE": MYTH OR REALITY?

1. Deborah M. Merrill, *Mothers-in-Law and Daughters-in-Law: Understanding the Relationship and What Makes Them Friends or Foe* (Westport, CT: Praeger Publishers, 2007).

2. *Salon*, http://letters.salon.com/mwt/broadsheet/2007/10/17/mother_in-law/view/index1.html?sh (retrieved 10/18/2007 and 10/19/2007).

3. Annette Lareau, *Unequal Childhoods: Class, Race, and Family Life* (Berkeley: University of California Press, 2003).

4. Karen V. Hansen, *Not-So-Nuclear Families: Class, Gender, and Networks of Care* (New Brunswick, NJ: Rutgers University Press, 2005).

5. Stephanie Coontz, *Marriage, a History: How Love Conquered Marriage* (New York: Penguin, 2005).

6. Merrill, *Mothers-in-Law and Daughters-in-Law*.

7. Nicholas W. Townsend, *The Package Deal: Marriage, Work, and Fatherhood in Men's Lives* (Philadelphia, PA: Temple University Press, 2002).

8. Jean Baker Miller, *Toward a New Psychology of Women* (Boston, MA: Beacon Press, 1986); Christina Robb, *This Changes Everything: The Relational Revolution in Psychology* (New York: Picador, 2007); Townsend, *The Package Deal.*

9. This was discussed in chapter 3.

6. THE EFFECT OF MARRIAGE ON INTERGENERATIONAL RELATIONSHIPS

1. Gayle Kaufman and Peter Uhlenberg, "Effects of Life Course Transitions on the Quality of Relationships between Adult Children and their Parents," *Journal of Marriage and Family* 60 (1998): 924–38.

2. William S. Aquilino, "From Adolescent to Young Adults: A Prospective Study of Parent-Child Relations during the Transition to Adulthood," *Journal of Marriage and Family* 59 (1997): 670–86.

3. Kaufman and Uhlenberg, "Effects of Life Course Transitions."

4. Kaufman and Uhlenberg, "Effects of Life Course Transitions.

5. Deborah M. Merrill, *Mothers-in-Law and Daughters-in-Law: Understanding the Relationship and What Makes Them Friends or Foe* (Westport, CT: Praeger Publishers, 2007).

6. Karen L. Fingerman, *Aging Mothers and Their Daughters: A Study of Mixed Emotions* (New York: Springer, 2001); Karen L. Fingerman, *Mothers and Their Adult Daughters* (Amherst, NY: Prometheus Books, 2003); Gunhild O. Hagestad, "The Family: Women and Grandparents as Kinkeepers," in *Our Aging Society* (New York: Norton, 1986), 141–60; Leora Lawton, Merril Silverstein, and Vern L. Bengtson, "Affection, Social Contact, and Geographic Distance between Adult Children and Their Parents," *Journal of Marriage and Family* 56 (1994): 57–68; Nadine F. Marks, "Midlife Marital Status Differences in Social Support Relationships with Adult Children and Psychological Well-Being," *Journal of Family Issues* 16 (1995): 5–28; Merril Silverstein, Tonya M. Parrott, and Vern L. Bengtson, "Factors that Predispose Middle-Aged Sons and Daughters to Provide Social Support to Older Parents," *Journal of Marriage and Family* 57 (1995): 465–75; Glenna Spitze and John Logan, "More Evidence on Women (and Men) in the Middle," *Research of Aging* 12 (1990): 182–98; Glenna Spitze and John Logan, "Sons, Daughters, and Intergenerational Social Support," *Journal of Marriage and Family* 52 (1990): 420–30.

7. Eungu Lee, Glenna Spitze, and John R. Logan, "Social Support to Parents-in-Law: The Interplay of Gender and Kin Hierarchies," *Journal of Marriage and Family* 65 (2003): 396–403.

8. Jean Baker Miller, *Toward a New Psychology of Women* (Boston, MA: Beacon Press, 1986); Christina Robb, *This Changes Everything: The Relational Revolution in Psychology* (New York: Picador, 2007).

9. M. Jean Turner, Carolyn R. Young, and Kelly I. Black, "Daughters-in-Law and Mothers-in-Law Seeking Their Place within the Family: A Qualitative Study of Differing Viewpoints," *Family Relations* 55 (2006): 588–600.

10. Nancy Chodorow, *The Reproduction of Mothering: Psychoanalysis and the Sociology of Gender* (Berkeley: University of California Press, 1978); Eva S. Lefkowitz and Karen L. Fingerman, "Positive and Negative Emotional Feelings and Behaviors in Mother-Daughter Ties in Late Life," *Journal of Family Psychology* 17 (2003): 607–17.

11. Miller, *Towards a New Psychology of Women*; Christine M. Proulx and Heather M. Helms, "Mothers' and Fathers' Perceptions of Change and Continuity in their Relationships with Young Adult Sons and Daughters," *Journal of Family Issues* 29, no. 2 (2008): 234–61; Robb, *This Changes Everything: The Relational Revolution in Psychology*.

12. Alice Rossi and Peter Rossi, *Of Human Bonding: Parent-Child Relations across the Life Course* (New York: Aldine de Gruyter, 1990).

13. Daphna Gans and Merril Silverstein, "Norms of Filial Responsibility for Aging Parents across Time and Generations," *Journal of Marriage and Family* 6, no. 4 (2006): 961–76.

14. Noelle Chesley and Kyle Poppie, "Assisting Parents and In-Laws: Gender, Type of Assistance, and Couple's Employment," *Journal of Marriage and Family* 71 (2009): 247–62.

15. Merril Silverstein, Tonya M. Parrott, and Vern L. Bengtson, "Factors That Predispose Middle-Aged Sons and Daughters to Provide Social Support to Older Parents," *Journal of Marriage and Family* 57 (1995): 465–75.

16. Nicholas W. Townsend, *The Package Deal: Marriage, Work, and Fatherhood in Men's Lives* (Philadelphia, PA: Temple University Press, 2002).

17. Deborah M. Merrill, *Caring for Elderly Parents: Juggling Work, Family and Caregiving in Middle and Working Class Families* (Westport, CT: Auburn House, 1997).

18. Miller, *Towards a New Psychology of Women*; Proulx and Helms, "Mothers' and Fathers' Perceptions of Change"; Robb, *This Changes Everything*.

7. THE CHALLENGE FOR MOTHERS IN PARENT–ADULT CHILD RELATIONSHIPS

1. Alice Rossi and Peter Rossi, *Of Human Bonding: Parent-Child Relations across the Life Course* (New York: Aldine de Gruyter, 1990); Arland Thornton, Terri L. Orbuch, and William G. Axinn, "Parent-Child Relations during the Transition to Adulthood," *Journal of Family Issues* 16 (1995): 538–64.

2. Leora Lawton, Merril Silverstein, and Vern L. Bengtson, "Affection, Social Contact, and Geographic Distance between Adult Children and Their Parents," *Journal of Marriage and Family* 56 (1994): 57–68; Nadine F. Marks, "Midlife Marital Status Differences in Social Support Relationships with Adult Children and Psychological Well-Being," *Journal of Family Issues* 16 (1995): 5–28; Merril Silverstein, Tonya M. Parrott, and Vern L. Bengtson, "Factors That Predispose Middle-Aged

Sons and Daughters to Provide Social Support to Older Parents," *Journal of Marriage and Family* 57 (1995): 465–75.

3. Russell A. Ward, Glenna Spitze, and Glenn Deane, "The More the Merrier? Multiple Parent–Adult Child Relations," *Journal of Marriage and Family* 71 (2009): 161–73.

4. Rossi and Rossi, *Of Human Bonding*.

5. Karen L. Fingerman, *Aging Mothers and Their Adult Daughters: A Study in Mixed Emotions* (New York: Springer, 2001); Karen L. Fingerman, *Mothers and Their Adult Daughters* (Amherst, NY: Prometheus Books, 2003); Gunhild O. Hagestad, "The Family: Women and Grandparents as Kinkeepers," in *Our Aging Society* (New York: Norton, 1986), 141–60; Glenna Spitze and John Logan, "More Evidence on Women (and Men) in the Middle," *Research on Aging* 12 (1990): 182–98.

6. Vern Bengtson, Carolyn Rosenthal, and Linda Burton, "Families and Aging: Diversity and Heterogeneity," in *Handbook of Aging and the Social Sciences* (San Diego, CA: Academic Press, 1990), 263–87; John R. Logan and Glenna D. Spitze, *Family Ties: Enduring Relations between Parents and their Grown Children* (Philadelphia, PA: Temple University Press, 1996); Diane Lye, "Adult Child–Parent Relationships," *Annual Review of Sociology* 22 (1996): 79–102; Phyllis Moen, "Gender, Age, and the Life Course," in *Handbook of Aging and the Social Sciences* (San Diego, CA: Academic Press, 1996), 171–87; Alice Rossi, "Intergenerational Relations: Gender, Norms, and Behavior," in *The Changing Contract across Generations* (New York: Aldine de Gruyter, 1993), 191–211; Merril Silverstein and Vern Bengtson, "Intergenerational Solidarity and the Structure of Adult Child–Parent Relationships in American Families," *American Journal of Sociology* 103 (1997): 429–60.

7. Frank F. Furstenberg and Andrew J. Cherlin, *Divided Families: What Happens to Children When Parents Part* (Cambridge, MA: Harvard University Press, 1991); Gunhild O. Hagestad, "The Family."

8. Silverstein, Parrott, and Bengtson, "Factors That Predispose Middle-Aged Sons and Daughters."

9. Merrill, *Mothers-in-Law and Daughters-in-Law*.

10. Merrill, *Mothers-in-Law and Daughters-in-Law*.

11. Andrea E. Willson, Kim M. Shuey, and Glenn H. Elder Jr., "Ambivalence in the Relationships of Adult Children to Aging Parents and In-Laws," *Journal of Marriage and Family* 65 (2003): 1055–72.

12. Gayle Kaufman and Peter Uhlenberg, "Effects of Life Course Transitions on the Quality of Relationships between Adult Children and Their Parents," *Journal of Marriage and Family* 60 (1998): 924–38.

13. Merrill, *Mothers-in-Law and Daughters-in-Law*.

14. Pamela Cotterill, *Friendly Relations? Mothers and Their Daughters-in-Law* (London: Taylor Francis, 1994); Lucy Rose Fischer, *Linked Lives: Adult Daughters and Their Mothers* (New York: Harper and Row Publishers, 1986); Merrill, *Mothers-in-Law and Daughters-in-Law*.

15. Merrill, *Mothers-in-Law and Daughters-in-Law*.

16. See chapter 3.

17. Eunju Lee, Glenna Spitze, and John R. Logan, "Social Support to Parents-in-Law: The Interplay of Gender and Kin Hierarchies," *Journal of Marriage and Family* 65 (2003): 396–403.
18. Merrill, *Mothers-in-Law and Daughters-in-Law.*
19. See chapter 3.
20. Furstenberg and Cherlin, *Divided Families*; Hagestad, "The Family."

8. THE EVOLUTION OF INTERGENERATIONAL RELATIONSHIPS FOLLOWING CHILDREN'S MARRIAGES

1. Gayle Kaufman and Peter Uhlenberg, "Effects of Life Course Transitions on the Quality of Relationships between Adult Children and Their Parents," *Journal of Marriage and Family* 60 (1998): 924–38.
2. William S. Aquilino, "From Adolescent to Young Adult: A Prospective Study of Parent-Child Relations during the Transition to Adulthood." *Journal of Marriage and Family* 59 (1997): 670–86.
3. Aquilino, "From Adolescent to Young Adult."
4. Natalia Sarkisian and Naomi Gerstel, "Till Marriage Do Us Part: Adult Children's Relationships with their Parents," *Journal of Marriage and Family* 70 (2008): 360–76.
5. Kaufman and Uhlenberg, "Effects of Life Course Transitions."
6. Kaufman and Uhlenberg, "Effects of Life Course Transitions."
7. Christine M. Proulx and Heather M. Helms, "Mothers' and Fathers' Perceptions of Change and Continuity in Their Relationships with Young Adult Sons and Daughters," *Journal of Family Issues* 29, no. 2 (2008): 234–61.
8. This refers to assistance with grocery shopping, paying bills, running errands, etc.
9. For a discussion of the effects of caregiving on parent-child relationships, see Deborah M. Merrill, *Caring for Elderly Parents: Juggling Work, Family, and Caregiving in Middle- and Working-Class Families* (Westport, CT: Auburn House, 1997).
10. Aquilino, "From Adolescent to Young Adult."
11. Aquilino, "From Adolescent to Young Adult"; Vern Bengtson and K. Black, "Solidarity between Parents and Children: Four Perspectives on Theory Development," paper presented at the Theory Development Workshop, National Council on Family Relations, Toronto, Canada (1973).

9. DIVORCE AND LATER-LIFE FAMILIES

1. Gayle Kaufman and Peter Uhlenberg, "Effects of Life Course Transitions on the Quality of Relationships between Adult Children and Their Parents," *Journal of Marriage and Family* 60 (1998): 924–38.

2. Merril Silverstein and Vern Bengtson, "Intergenerational Solidarity and the Structure of Adult Child-Parent Relationships in American Families," *American Journal of Sociology* 103 (1997): 429–60.

3. Kaufman and Uhlenberg, "Effects of Life Course Transitions."

4. Natalia Sarkisian and Naomi Gerstel, "Till Marriage Do Us Part: Adult Children's Relationships with Their Parents," *Journal of Marriage and Family* 70 (2008): 360–76.

5. Glenna Spitze, John Logan, Glenn Deane, and Suzanne Zerger, "Adult Children's Divorce and Intergenerational Relationships," *Journal of Marriage and Family* 56 (1994): 279–93.

6. Karl Pillemer and J. Jill Suitor, "Exploring Mothers' Ambivalence toward Their Adult Children," *Journal of Marriage and Family* 64 (2002): 602–13.

7. Katie's ex-husband was not the father of her daughter.

8. Spitze, Logan, Deane, and Zerger, "Adult Children's Divorce."

9. Kaufman and Uhlenberg, "Effects of Life Course Transitions"; Sarkisian and Gerstel, "Till Marriage Do Us Part."

11. RECIPROCAL EFFECTS: HOW DO INTERGENERATIONAL RELATIONSHIPS AFFECT ADULT CHILDREN'S MARRIAGES?

1. Paul R. Amato, Alan Booth, David R. Johnson, and Stacy J. Rogers, *Alone Together: How Marriage in America Is Changing* (Cambridge, MA: Harvard University Press, 2007); Andrew Cherlin, *The Marriage-Go-Round: The State of Marriage and the Family Today* (New York: Alfred A. Knopf, 2009).

2. Deborah M. Merrill, *Mothers-in-Law and Daughters-in-Law: Understanding the Relationship and What Makes Them Friends or Foe* (Westport, CT: Praeger Publishers, 2007); Susan Shapiro Barash, *Mothers-in-Law and Daughters-in-Law: Love, Hate, Rivalry and Reconciliation* (Far Hills, NJ: New Horizon Press, 2001).

3. Centers for Disease Control, FastStats, Marriage and Divorce, accessed June 1, 2010, http://www.cdc.gov/nchs/fastats/divorce.htm.

12. CONCLUSION

1. Deborah M. Merrill, *Mothers-in-Law and Daughters-in-Law: Understanding the Relationship and What Makes Them Friends or Foe* (Westport, CT: Praeger Publishers, 2007).

2. *Salon*, http://letters.salon.com/mwt/broadsheet/2007/10/17/mother_in_law/view/index1.html?sh (retrieved 10/18/2007 and 10/19/2007).

3. Russell A. Ward, Glenna Spitze, and Glenn Deane, "The More the Merrier? Multiple Parent–Adult Child Relations," *Journal of Marriage and Family* 71 (2009): 161–73.

4. Eunju Lee, Glenna Spitze, and John R. Logan, "Social Support to Parents-in-Law: The Interplay of Gender and Kin Hierarchies," *Journal of Marriage and Family* 65 (2003): 396–403.

158 *Notes*

5. Nicholas W. Townsend, *The Package Deal: Marriage, Work, and Fatherhood in Men's Lives* (Philadelphia, PA: Temple University Press, 2002).

6. Karen V. Hansen, *Not-So-Nuclear Families: Class, Gender, and Networks of Care* (New Brunswick, NJ: Rutgers University Press, 2005).

7. Nancy Chodorow, *The Reproduction of Mothering: Psychoanalysis and the Sociology of Gender* (Berkeley: University of California Press, 1978); Karen L. Fingerman, *Aging Mothers and Their Adult Daughters: A Study in Mixed Emotions* (New York: Springer, 2001); Karen L. Fingerman, *Mothers and Their Adult Daughters* (Amherst, NY: Prometheus Books, 2003).

8. Jean Baker Miller, *Toward a New Psychology of Women* (Boston, MA: Beacon Press, 1986); Christina Robb, *This Changes Everything: The Relational Revolution in Psychology* (New York: Picador, 2007).

9. Merrill, *Mothers-in-Law and Daughters-in-Law.*

10. James V. Cordova, Rogina L. Scott, Marina Dorian, Shilagh Mirgain, Daniel Yaeger, and Allison Groot, "The Marriage Check-Up: A Motivational Interview Approach to the Promotion of Marital Health with Couples At-Risk for Relationship Deterioration, " *Behavior Therapy* 36 (2005): 301–10.

11. Deborah M. Merrill, *Caring for Elderly Parents: Juggling Work, Family and Caregiving in Middle and Working Class Families* (Westport, CT: Auburn House, 1997).

12. Other researchers have found that not only is there variation in relationships within families, but that mothers actually have "favorites" among their children. See: J. Jill Suitor, and Karl Pillemer, "Choosing Daughters: Exploring Why Mothers Favor Adult Daughters over Sons," *Sociological Perspectives* 49, no. 2 (2006): 221–30; J. Jill Suitor, Jori Sechrist, and Karl Pillemer, "Within Family Differences in Mothers' Support to Adult Children," *Journal of Gerontology: Social Sciences* 16B (2006): S10–7; J. Jill Suitor, Jori Sechrist, Michael Steinhour, and Karl Pillemer, "'I'm Sure She Chose Me!' Accuracy of Children's Reports of Mothers' Favoritism in Later Life Families," *Family Relations* 55, no. 5 (2006): 526–38.

13. Ann Goetting, "Patterns of Support among In-Laws in the United States," *Journal of Family Issues* 1, no. 1 (1990): 67–90; Lee, Spitze, and Logan, "Social Support to Parents-in-Law"; Kim Shuey and Melissa Hardy, "Assistance to Aging Parents and Parents-in-Law: Does Lineage Affect Family Allocation Decisions?" *Journal of Marriage and Family* 65 (2003): 418–31.

14. Gayle Kaufman and Peter Uhlenberg, "Effects of Life Course Transitions on the Quality of Relationships between Adult Children and Their Parents," *Journal of Marriage and Family* 60 (1998): 924–38.

15. See Ingrid A. Connidis, *Family Ties and Aging*, 2nd ed. (Thousand Oaks, CA: Sage Publications, 2010) for an overview of the research.

16. Hansen, *Not-So-Nuclear Families.*

17. Stephanie Coontz, *Marriage, a History: How Love Conquered Marriage* (New York: Penguin, 2005).

18. Paul Amato, "Tension between Institutional and Individual Views of Marriage," *Journal of Marriage and Family* 66 (2004): 959–65; Paul R. Amato, Alan Booth, David R. Johnson, and Stacy J. Rogers. *Alone Together: How Marriage in*

America is Changing (Cambridge, MA: Harvard University Press, 2007); Andrew Cherlin, "The Deinstitutionalization of American Marriage," *Journal of Marriage and Family* 66 (2004): 848–61; Andrew Cherlin, *The Marriage-Go-Round: The State of Marriage and the Family in America Today* (New York: Alfred A. Knopf, 2009); Coontz, *Marriage, a History*.

19. Miller, *Toward a New Psychology of Women*; Robb, *This Changes Everything*.

20. Connidis, *Family Ties and Aging*.

21. Kathryn Edin and Maria Kefalas, *Promises I Can Keep* (Berkeley: University of California Press, 2005).

Bibliography

Aldous, Joan. "New Views of Grandparents in Intergenerational Context." *Journal of Family Issues* 16 (1995): 104–22.

Allen, Katherine R., Rosemary Blieszner, and Karen A. Roberto. "Families in the Middle and Later Years: A Review and Critique of Research in the 1990s." *Journal of Marriage and Family* 62 (2000): 911–26.

Amato, Paul. "Tension between Institutional and Individual Views of Marriage." *Journal of Marriage and Family* 66 (2004): 959–65.

Amato, Paul R., Alan Booth, David R. Johnson, and Stacy J. Rogers. *Alone Together: How Marriage in America Is Changing.* Cambridge, MA: Harvard University Press, 2007.

Aquilino, William S. "From Adolescent to Young Adult: A Prospective Study of Parent-Child Relations during the Transition to Adulthood." *Journal of Marriage and Family* 59 (1997): 670–86.

———. "Two Views of One Relationship: Comparing Parents' and Young Adult Children's Reports on the Quality of Intergenerational Relationships." *Journal of Marriage and Family* 61 (1999): 858–70.

Bengtson, Vern, and K. Black. "Solidarity between Parents and Children: Four Perspectives on Theory Development." Paper presented at the Theory Development Workshop, National Council on Family Relations, Toronto, Canada, 1973.

Bengtson, Vern, Carolyn Rosenthal, and Linda Burton. "Families and Aging: Diversity and Heterogeneity." In *Handbook of Aging and the Social Sciences*, edited by Robert Binstock and Linda George, 3rd ed., 263–87. San Diego, CA: Academic Press, 1990.

Bengtson, Vern, Timothy Biblarz, and Robert Roberts. *How Families Still Matter: A Longitudinal Study of Youth in Two Generations.* New York: Cambridge University Press, 2002.

Booth, Alan, and Paul R. Amato. "Parental Marital Quality, Parental Divorce, and Relations with Parents." *Journal of Marriage and Family* 56 (1994): 21–34.

Cherlin, Andrew. "The Deinstitutionalization of American Marriage." *Journal of Marriage and Family* 66 (2004): 848–61.

161

———. *The Marriage-Go-Round: The State of Marriage and the Family in America To-day*. New York: Alfred A. Knopf, 2009.

Chesley, Noelle, and Kyle Poppie. "Assisting Parents and In-Laws: Gender, Type of Assistance, and Couple's Employment." *Journal of Marriage and Family* 71 (2009): 247–62.

Chodorow, Nancy. *The Reproduction of Mothering: Psychoanalysis and the Sociology of Gender*. Berkeley: University of California Press, 1978.

Climo, Jacob. *Distant Parents*. New Brunswick, NJ: Rutgers University Press, 1992.

Coleman, Marilyn, Larry Ganong, and Susan M. Cable. "Beliefs about Women's Intergenerational Family Obligations to Provide Support Before and After Divorce and Remarriage." *Journal of Marriage and Family* 56 (1997): 165–76.

Coleman, Marilyn, Larry H. Ganong, and Tanya C. Rothrauff. "Racial and Ethnic Similarities and Differences in Beliefs about Intergenerational Assistance to Older Adults after Divorce and Remarriage." *Family Relations* 55 (2006): 576–87.

Connidis, Ingrid A. *Family Ties and Aging*. Thousand Oaks, CA: Sage Publications, 2001.

———. *Family Ties and Aging*. 2nd ed. Thousand Oaks, CA: Sage Publications, 2010.

Coontz, Stephanie. *Marriage, a History: How Love Conquered Marriage*. New York: Penguin, 2005.

Cordova, James V., Rogina L. Scott, Marina Dorian, Shilagh Mirgain, Daniel Yaeger, and Allison Groot. "The Marriage Checkup: A Motivational Interview Approach to the Promotion of Marital Health with Couples At-Risk for Relationship Deterioration." *Behavior Therapy* 36 (2005): 301–10.

Coser, Lewis, and Rose Coser. *Greedy Institutions: Patterns of Undivided Commitment*. New York: Free Press, 1974.

Cotterill, Pamela. *Friendly Relations? Mothers and Their Daughters-in-Law*. London: Taylor-Francis, 1994.

Edin, Kathryn, and Maria Kefalas. *Promises I Can Keep*. Berkeley: University of California Press, 2005.

Elder, Glen H., Jr., Laura L. Rudkin, and Rand D. Conger. "Intergenerational Continuity and Change in Rural America." In *Adult Intergenerational Relations: Effects of Societal Change*, edited by Vern L. Bengtson, K. Warner Schaie, and Linda M. Burton, 30–60. New York: Springer, 1995.

Fingerman, Karen L. *Aging Mothers and Their Adult Daughters: A Study in Mixed Emotions*. New York: Springer, 2001.

———. *Mothers and Their Adult Daughters*. Amherst, NY: Prometheus Books, 2003.

Fingerman, Karen L., Elizabeth Hay, and Kira S. Birditt. "The Best of Ties, the Worst of Ties: Close, Problematic, and Ambivalent Social Relationships." *Journal of Marriage and Family* 66 (2004): 792–808.

Fischer, Claude. *America Calling: A Social History of the Telephone to 1940*. Berkeley: University of California Press, 1992.

Fischer, Lucy Rose. *Linked Lives: Adult Daughters and Their Mothers*. New York: Harper and Row Publishers, 1986.

Frank, Susan J., Catherine B. Avery, and Mark S. Laman. "Young Adults Perceptions of Their Relationships with Their Parents: Individual Differences in Connectedness, Competence, and Emotional Autonomy." *Developmental Psychology* 24 (1988): 729–37.

Furstenberg, Frank F., and Andrew J. Cherlin. *Divided Families: What Happens to Children When Parents Part.* Cambridge, MA: Harvard University Press, 1991.

Gans, Daphna, and Merril Silverstein. "Norms of Filial Responsibility for Aging Parents across Time and Generations." *Journal of Marriage and Family* 68, no. 4 (2006): 961–76.

Gilligan, Carol. *In a Different Voice: Psychological Theory and Women's Development.* Cambridge, MA: Harvard University Press, 1982.

Goetting, Ann. "Patterns of Support among In-Laws in the United States. *Journal of Family Issues* 11, no. 1 (1990): 67–90.

Hagestad, Gunhild O. "Dimensions of Time and Family." *American Behavioral Scientist* 29 (1986): 679–94.

———. "The Family: Women and Grandparents as Kinkeepers." In *Our Aging Society*, edited by A. Pifer and L. Bronte, 141–60. New York: Norton, 1986.

Hansen, Karen V. *Not-So-Nuclear Families: Class, Gender, and Networks of Care.* New Brunswick, NJ: Rutgers University Press, 2005.

Jordan, Judith V. *Relational-Cultural Therapy.* Washington, DC: American Psychological Association, 2009.

Kaufman, Gayle, and Peter Uhlenberg. "Effects of Life Course Transitions on the Quality of Relationships between Adult Children and Their Parents." *Journal of Marriage and Family* 60 (1998): 924–38.

Laureau, Annette. *Unequal Childhoods: Class, Race, and Family Life.* Berkeley: University of California Press, 2003.

Lawton, Leora, Merril Silverstein, and Vern L. Bengtson. "Solidarity between Generations in Families." In *Intergenerational Linkages: Hidden Connections in American Society*, edited by Vern L. Bengtson and Robert A. Harootyan, 19–42. New York: Springer Publishers, 1994.

———. "Affection, Social Contact, and Geographic Distance between Adult Children and Their Parents." *Journal of Marriage and Family* 56 (1994): 57–68.

Lee, Eunju, Glenna Spitze, and John R. Logan. "Social Support to Parents-in-Law: The Interplay of Gender and Kin Hierarchies." *Journal of Marriage and Family* 65 (2003): 396–403.

Lefkowitz, Eva S., and Karen L. Fingerman. "Positive and Negative Emotional Feelings and Behaviors in Mother-Daughter Ties in Late Life." *Journal of Family Psychology* 17 (2003): 607–17.

Lin, Ge, and Peter Rogerson. "Elderly Parents and the Geographic Availability of Their Adult Children." *Research on Aging* 17, no. 3 (1995): 303–31.

Logan, John R., and Glenna D. Spitze. *Family Ties: Enduring Relations between Parents and Their Grown Children.* Philadelphia, PA: Temple University Press, 1996.

Lye, Diane. "Adult Child–Parent Relationships." *Annual Review of Sociology* 22 (1996): 79–102.

Marks, Nadine F. "Midlife Marital Status Differences in Social Support Relationships with Adult Children and Psychological Well-Being." *Journal of Family Issues* 16 (1995): 5–28.

Merrill, Deborah M. *Caring for Elderly Parents: Juggling Work, Family, and Caregiving in Middle- and Working-Class Families*. Westport, CT: Auburn House, 1997.

———. *Mothers-in-Law and Daughters-in-Law: Understanding the Relationship and What Makes Them Friends or Foe*. Westport, CT: Praeger Publishers, 2007.

Miller, Jean Baker. *Toward a New Psychology of Women*. Boston, MA: Beacon Press, 1986.

Moen, Phyllis. "Gender, Age, and the Life Course." In *Handbook of Aging and the Social Sciences*, edited by Robert Binstock and Linda George, 4th ed., 171–87. San Diego, CA: Academic Press, 1996.

Pillemer, Karl, and J. Jill Suitor. (2002). "Exploring Mothers' Ambivalence toward Their Adult Children." *Journal of Marriage and Family* 64 (2002): 602–13.

Proulx, Christine M., and Heather M. Helms. "Mothers' and Fathers' Perceptions of Change and Continuity in Their Relationships with Young Adult Sons and Daughters." *Journal of Family Issues* 29, no. 2 (2008): 234–61.

Robb, Christina. *This Changes Everything: The Relational Revolution in Psychology*. New York: Picador, 2007.

Rossi, Alice. "Intergenerational Relations: Gender, Norms, and Behavior." In *The Changing Contract across Generations*, edited by Vern L. Bengtson and William Achenbaum, 191–211. New York: Aldine de Gruyter, 1993.

Rossi, Alice, and Peter Rossi. *Of Human Bonding: Parent-Child Relations across the Life Course*. New York: Aldine de Gruyter, 1990.

Salon. http://letters.salon.com/mwt/broadsheet/2007/10/17/mother_in_law/view/index1html?sh (Retrieved 10/18/2007 and 10/19/2007).

Sarkisian, Natalia, and Naomi Gerstel. "Till Marriage Do Us Part: Adult Children's Relationships with Their Parents." *Journal of Marriage and Family* 70 (2008): 360–76.

Shuey, Kim, and Melissa Hardy. "Assistance to Aging Parents and Parents-in-Law: Does Lineage Affect Family Allocation Decisions?" *Journal of Marriage and Family* 65 (2003): 418–31.

Silverstein, Merril, and Vern Bengtson. "Intergenerational Solidarity and the Structure of Adult Child–Parent Relationships in American Families." *American Journal of Sociology* 103 (1997): 429–60.

Silverstein, Merril, Tonya M. Parrott, and Vern L. Bengtson. "Factors That Predispose Middle-Aged Sons and Daughters to Provide Social Support to Older Parents." *Journal of Marriage and Family* 57 (1995): 465–75.

Spitze, Glenna, and John Logan. "More Evidence on Women (and Men) in the Middle." *Research on Aging* 12 (1990): 182–98.

———. "Sons, Daughters, and Intergenerational Social Support." *Journal of Marriage and Family* 52 (1990): 420–30.

———. "Sibling Structure and Intergenerational Relations." *Journal of Marriage and Family* 53 (1991): 871–84.

———. "Employment and Filial Relations: Is There a Conflict?" *Sociological Forum* 6 (1991): 681–97.

Spitze, Glenna, John Logan, Glenn Deane, and Suzanne Zerger. "Adult Children's Divorce and Intergenerational Relationships." *Journal of Marriage and Family* 56 (1994): 279–93.

Suitor, J. Jill, and Karl Pillemer. "Choosing Daughters: Exploring Why Mothers Favor Adult Daughters over Sons." *Sociological Perspectives* 49, no. 2 (2006): 221–30.

Suitor, J. Jill, Jori Sechrist, and Karl Pillemer. "Within Family Differences in Mothers' Support to Adult Children." *Journal of Gerontology: Social Sciences* 16B (2006): S10-7.

Suitor, J. Jill, Jori Sechrist, Michael Steinhour, and Karl Pillemer. "'I'm Sure She Chose Me!' Accuracy of Children's Reports of Mothers' Favoritism in Later-Life Families." *Family Relations* 55, no. 5 (2006): 526–38.

Thornton, Arland, Terri L. Orbuch, and William G. Axinn. "Parent-Child Relations during the Transition to Adulthood." *Journal of Family Issues* 16 (1995): 538–64.

Townsend, Nicholas W. *The Package Deal: Marriage, Work, and Fatherhood in Men's Lives.* Philadelphia, PA: Temple University Press, 2002.

Turner, M. Jean, Carolyn R. Young, and Kelly I. Black. "Daughters-in-Law and Mothers-in-Law Seeking Their Place within the Family: A Qualitative Study of Differing Viewpoints." *Family Relations* 55 (2006): 588–600.

Umberson, Debra. "Relationships between Adult Children and Their Parents: Psychological Consequences for Both Generations." *Journal of Marriage and Family* 54 (1992): 664–74.

Waite, Linda, and Maggie Gallagher. *The Case for Marriage: Why Married People Are Happier, Healthier, and Better Off Financially.* New York: Doubleday, 2000.

Ward, Russell A., Glenna Spitze, and Glenn Deane. "The More the Merrier? Multiple Parent–Adult Child Relations." *Journal of Marriage and Family* 71 (2009): 161–73.

Willson, Andrea E., Kim M. Shuey, and Glenn H. Elder Jr. "Ambivalence in the Relationships of Adult Children to Aging Parents and In-Laws." *Journal of Marriage and Family* 65 (2003): 1055–72.

Index

About the Author

Deborah M. Merrill is an associate professor of sociology at Clark University. Her areas of specialization are families, aging, medicine, and research methodology. Her previous books include *Caring for Elderly Parents: Juggling Work, Family, and Caregiving in Middle and Working Class Families* (1997) and *Mothers-in-Law and Daughters-in-Law: Understanding the Relationship and What Makes Them Friends or Foe* (2007).